# Smart
# Pressure Cooker
# Recipes

## Carol Heding Munson

**Sterling Publishing Co., Inc.**
New York

A hearty thank you to Russell and Roger, who critiqued every recipe and enthusiastically offered opinions. And a loving thank you to Lowell for his invaluable assistance and encouragement with recipe and manuscript development and his cheerful handling of the daily supermarket shuttle.

**Library of Congress Cataloging-in-Publication Data**

Munson, Carol.
    Smart pressure cooker recipes / Carol Heding Munson.
       p.   cm.
    Includes index.
    ISBN 0-8069-9985-3
    1. Pressure cookery.   I. Title.
TX840.P7M86       1998
641.5'87–dc21

                                         98-3368
                                           CIP

10  9  8  7  6  5  4  3

Published by Sterling Publishing Company, Inc.
387 Park Avenue South, New York, N.Y. 10016
© 1998 by Carol Heding Munson
Distributed in Canada by Sterling Publishing
℅ Canadian Manda Group, One Atlantic Avenue, Suite 105
Toronto, Ontario, Canada M6K 3E7
Distributed in Great Britain and Europe by Cassell PLC
Wellington House, 125 Strand, London WC2R 0BB, England
Distributed in Australia by Capricorn Link (Australia) Pty Ltd.
P.O. Box 6651, Baulkham Hills, Business Centre, NSW 2153, Australia
*Manufactured in the United States of America*
*All rights reserved*

Sterling ISBN 0-8069-9985-3

# Contents

# Preface

I knew I'd found a great way to serve up fresh food fast the minute I tasted the roast, which was tender and flavorful with a rich dark mushroom gravy, everything a succulent piece of meat should be.

But I wanted to be sure. Was the technique really fast? So I whipped up Black Bean and Corn Chili with home-cooked beans (not the canned variety that's loaded with sodium). It was ready to eat in minutes and tasted superb, just as if the beans had simmered for hours. Amazing. I could start making dinner at 5 o'clock and sit down to eat about 6.

Good show, but one more quick test: I tried my hand at a Chocolate-Chip Cheesecake Dessert. It was done on the double and turned out to be a luscious chocoholic's delight. Hmm, I could whisk together a spur-of-the-moment dessert early on Sunday and have it thoroughly chilled and set by brunch.

My speed-cooking technique: a pressure cooker.

Pressure cooking isn't new, of course. But it's something I hadn't really tried until about two years ago. And I was sold, sold on creating family-favorite meals that are fast, fantastic tasting, and fit for diet-wise eating, to boot. In the following pages, I share 80 palate-pleasing recipes that have withstood the rigors of cooking under pressure—when I'm under pressure to get things done fast.

# Under Pressure

When you think about it, the pressure cooker is a pretty amazing pot. It'll simmer up a comforting corned beef and cabbage dinner, complete with the requisite potatoes, in about an hour or steam a trendy jerk turkey breast to perfection in less than 50 minutes.

Thinking more along the lines of a thick, flavorful potato soup? A pressure cooker can have the potatoes ready for pureeing after just 6 minutes of cooking. Or how about soul-satisfying chicken rice soup? Or a robust bean and pasta soup? Both cook in less than 20 minutes.

And if your mouth is watering for a smooth custardy pudding, a pudding lush with ripe bananas and topped with pure maple syrup, the cooker can steam it in just 20 minutes, including the time to release the pressure.

## HOW PRESSURE COOKERS WORK

Pressure cookers aren't all that new. In fact, they've been marketed in the U.S. since before World War II and were extremely popular for preparing quick home-style meals during the '50s and early '60s. A youngster in those years, I can remember watching my mother on more than one hot summer's evening stuff the cooker with fresh corn on the cob. Minutes later she'd serve the ears, steaming hot and dripping with melted butter, along with potato salad and cold chicken that she'd prepared earlier in the day. In cold weather, she'd use the cooker to stew up a stick-to-your-ribs beef, potato and carrot dinner. And it was ready so fast I thought it was magic. Nowadays, in our search for speedy ways to get dinner on the double, interest in this handy kitchen tool has been rekindled.

Though today's PCs (that's...er, pressure cookers, not personal computers) look slicker and allow for more accurate timing than earlier models, the scientific principle under which they achieve quick results remains the same: They seal in steam by means of a rubber gasket that's locked between the lid and the pot itself, raising the pressure within the cooker. As the pressure goes up, so does the boiling point of water. Normally water boils at 212°F (100°C); under 15 pounds of pressure (the amount created within a pressure cooker), it boils at 250°F (121°C). And hotter temperatures mean faster cooking.

There are three designs of pressure cookers: first-generation, or jiggle tops; second-generation, with pressure indicator rods; and newer jiggle tops that are quieter. The jiggle tops use a weight balanced on a pipe vent to indicate when they're reached 15 pounds of pressure, at which point the weight rocks, audibly emitting excess steam. Second-generation cookers set pressure using a spring-valve design and a rod that shows the actual pressure. All pressure cookers require adjusting the stove's heat under the PC to maintain steady pressure.

## WHAT TO LOOK FOR IN A PRESSURE COOKER

In the market for a new cooker? Then consider getting a big one. This is why: Foods often expand during cooking, but even if they don't, cookers need room for pressure to build. The consequences are that you can fill pressure cookers only about half full for beans and two-thirds for other dishes.

My recommendation: Go for a six-quart. That's the size used for testing the recipes here and it's ideal for cooking soups and stews that serve four to six people; anything smaller may be too limiting. If you're thinking of making lots of stock, however, or if you frequently cook for a crowd, better get an 8- or 10-quart.

## SAFETY UNDER PRESSURE

Maybe it's because pressure cookers gurgle, hiss, and clank as they cook or maybe it's because of wild, unproven tales, but some cooks fear pressure cookers, thinking the noisy gizmos might explode. Relax. There's nothing to worry about. Modern pressure cookers are completely safe. They come equipped with these fail-proof safety features:

*An overpressure plug or a backup vent.* This releases pressure and keeps it from going too high if you forget to turn down the heat or if the pipe vent accidentally becomes clogged with food. Replace the rubber plug (it's inexpensive to purchase and easy to change) when it becomes sticky, cracked or dry.

*A locking lid.* This must be secured before pressure will rise. If the lid isn't locked, the pot functions like an everyday, unpressurized pot.

*A rubber seal.* This gasket, which expands as the cooker heats up, keeps steam in the pot as the pressure mounts. And it locks the lid in place until all the pressure has been released. If you ever have difficulty opening your cooker, wait a minute or two for any remaining pressure to dissipate. Try again; opening should be easy. Replace the gasket (they're available mail-order from the manufacturer) when it becomes sticky, cracked or dry.

## GETTING THE MOST FROM YOUR PRESSURE COOKER

For guaranteed superb results every time you cook under pressure, follow these simple guidelines:

*Read the instructions that came with your pressure cooker.* Every model is different, and you'll need to know how to fasten the lid, build and maintain pressure, and release pressure.

*Keep the vent pipe clear.* It's easy to do. After every use, simply clean the vent pipe with a pipe cleaner, skinny brush or toothpick. A clear pipe means an efficient cooker.

*Cut meat, poultry, and vegetables into uniform pieces.* This insures that all pieces will be done at the same time.

*Add seasonings in stages:* some at the beginning of cooking, others reserved for a finishing touch. Spices such as turmeric, cumin, and coriander, can easily withstand lots of heat, and cooking, which will eliminate any raw taste, actually develops their special flavors. Add them at the start of cooking. Delicate herbs like basil, dill, marjoram, and cilantro are heat-sensitive; stir them in at serving time for a burst of captivating flavor.

*Fill the cooker only half to two-thirds full.* Why? Your pressure cooker needs room, at least a third of the pot, for foods to expand and for pressure to build. Foods touching the lid make the cooker less efficient.

*Avoid foods that foam.* These include ingredients that usually get frothy and boil over in everyday stove-top cooking: pasta, rice, oatmeal, pearl barley, other grains, split peas, lentils, rhubarb and cranberries, to name a few. In the PC, they can clog the vent pipe and overpressure plug. For a precise list of what not to prepare in your model cooker, see the manufacturer's directions.

Having said that, I must add another note of caution. Avoid cooking rice in the PC. The instructions with my cooker included several rice recipes, but cooking rice, even a very small amount of it in a thin soup, gave me a surprise: The cooker spit and sputtered and the jiggle top ceased to rock (without the temperature being lowered). Sensing a problem, I removed the cooker from the heat. When everything cooled down, I inspected the lid. Sure enough, pieces of rice and debris had jammed the vent.

Some cookbooks say that adding oil or butter will keep foaming under control; proceed with care. To sidestep the problem altogether, simply use cooked rice and add it to soups and stews at the end of pressure cooking. That's what I now do.

*Use the amount of liquid recommended for your cooker.* Some cookers need only ½ cup; others require as much as 2 cups for producing steam pressure. Liquids include stocks, broth, juices, water and tomato sauce. Oil is not considered a liquid.

## COOKING MEATS AND POULTRY

There's no mistaking the power of a pressure cooker for turning lean meats and poultry into tender, delectable morsels in no time flat. Pot roasts and corned beef are fork-tender in 45 minutes; stews are done in just 10 to 15.

For subtle added flavor, I usually brown (a technique called braising) meats and poultry in a skillet, and then transfer them to a pressure cooker before adding other ingredients and bringing everything up to pressure. Thus, you'll find a goodly number of recipes in this book that specify sautéing as the first step. When browning, stop as the food turns golden brown, a stage that yields palate-pleasing flavor and eye-appealing color.

## COOKING VEGETABLES

The first thing you'll notice about cooking vegetables in a pressure cooker is that they're done in nanoseconds—at least, it seems that fast. Here are my suggestions for handling the speed: If you enjoy eating broccoli, cauliflower, summer squash and other tender vegetables at the slightly crisp stage, steam them on a rack and keep timing very brief, almost to nothing. Give heartier vegetables like potatoes, carrots, sweet potatoes, and winter squash a quick simmer in a flavorful broth; they respond beautifully. To help you estimate cooking times, I've devised the table on page 9.

**Note:** Timing starts as soon as the cooker reaches pressure. Quick-release the pressure at the end of the minimum time. If the vegetables are slightly underdone, replace the lid, but don't lock it, and finish cooking without pressure.

## VEGETABLE COOKING TIMES

| Vegetable (1 Pound) | Approximate Time* (Minutes) |
|---|---|
| Acorn squash | 2 to 4 |
| Asparagus** | Remove from heat as soon as pressure is reached |
| Beets | 3 to 5 |
| Broccoli** | Remove from heat as soon as pressure is reached |
| Brussels sprouts | 2 to 3 |
| Butternut squash | 3 to 5 |
| Carrots | 4 to 6 |
| Cauliflower** | Remove from heat as soon as pressure is reached |
| Corn** | 1 to 3 |
| Green beans | 1 to 3 |
| Leeks | 1 to 3 |
| Potatoes | 5 to 8 |
| Summer squash | Remove from heat as soon as pressure is reached |
| Turnips | 3 to 5 |
| Sweet potatoes | 4 to 7 |
| Zucchini | Remove from heat as soon as pressure is reached |

*Times are approximate and will vary depending on your pressure cooker and stove.

**Cook on a rack over water.

## COOKING BEANS

I'm absolutely convinced there is no better way to cook beans than in a pressure cooker. They emerge tender and flavorful and packed with the usual good-for-you fiber. They're done in a flash and have none of the glop and excessive sodium found in the canned products.

There are two equally delicious ways to prepare easily digested beans:

1. Soak beans in cold water to cover in a glass bowl in your refrigera-

tor for 12 to 24 hours. Drain the beans and place them in your pressure cooker; follow the instructions under "for either method" below. OR

2. Place beans in water to cover in your pressure cooker. Place the lid on the cooker, but don't lock it in place. Bring the water to a boil and remove the cooker from the heat. Soak the beans for an hour; drain them. Return the beans to the cooker; follow the instructions under "for either method" below.

**For either method:** Cover the beans with at least an inch of water (or add liquid and seasonings according to the directions in a specific recipe). Place the lid on the cooker, lock it into position, and place the pressure regulator on the vent pipe if you're using a first-generation cooker. Over medium-high or high heat, bring the cooker up to pressure. Then, lower the heat, adjusting it as necessary to maintain pressure (regulator should rock gently), and cook the beans until they're tender. See the timetable below for approximate times.

**Note:** Timing starts as soon as the cooker reaches pressure. Quick-release the pressure at the end of the minimum time. If beans are

### BEAN COOKING TIMES

| BEANS (1 CUP) | APPROXIMATE TIME* (MINUTES) |
| --- | --- |
| Black beans | 9 to 11 |
| Black-eyed peas | 5 to 8 |
| Chickpeas (garbanzos) | 11 to 15 |
| Kidney beans | 9 to 12 |
| Lentils | Not recommended |
| Limas | Not recommended |
| Navy beans | 5 to 8 |
| Pinto | 5 to 8 |
| Red chili beans | 9 to 11 |
| Split peas | Not recommended |
| White beans (Great Northern) | 5 to 8 |

*After soaking in cold water for 12–24 hours or in hot water for 1 hour.

slightly underdone, replace the lid, but don't lock it, and finish cooking without pressure.

## HOW TO READ THE RECIPES

Because pressure cooking is unique, it has its own recipe language. To help you become PC savvy fast, here's an explanation of the phrases used in the recipe directions in this book.

*Place a rack or trivet in a pressure cooker.* Most cookers come with a rack; some of the newer ones even include a steaming basket. If yours didn't come so equipped, use a small wire cooling rack or a metal trivet instead.

*Lock lid into position.* To do this, follow the manufacturer's instructions. The lid must be closed properly for pressure to rise.

*Place the pressure regulator on the vent pipe.* This step is necessary only if you have a jiggle-top cooker.

*Over medium-high or high heat, bring the cooker up to pressure.* Depending on the quantity of food in the cooker, the temperature of the ingredients, and your stove, bringing the cooker up to pressure can take anywhere from 1 to 30 minutes. Your goal is to get pressure up to 15 pounds as quickly as possible, but you shouldn't exceed the heat recommendation in your instruction booklet; some manufacturers advise against using high heat on electric stoves. **Helpful hint:** You can start warming large quantities of liquid while you're chopping and sautéing other ingredients to add to your cooker. Begin timing as soon as pressure is reached.

*Lower the heat, adjusting it as necessary to maintain pressure (regulator should rock gently).* Exactly how much to reduce the heat depends on your stove and cooker. After using the cooker a few times, you'll know approximately which temperature setting will maintain pressure.

*Let the pressure drop naturally.* When cooking time is up, remove your cooker from the heat and let it sit until the pressure drops completely. How long should it rest? That depends on the quantity of food and your cooker, but a full pot of soup may take 15 to 20 minutes. Remember, food continues to cook while the pressure drops.

*Quick-release the pressure.* When a recipe advises a quick-release for vegetables that require brief cooking, bring down the pressure by holding the cooker under cold running water or by placing it in a sinkful of cold water, if you have a jiggle-top cooker. On cookers with a spring-valve system, use the release valve as instructed in your manual—unless using it produces a spray of hot steam. If it does, revert to the cold water method. **Helpful hint:** Don't let water run over the backup vent (overpressure plug).

Carefully remove the pressure regulator and lid. There's steam, although not a lot, in the cooker even after the pressure has been released, so stay cool (and safe): tilt the cooker away as you take off the jiggle top and then the lid.

## ADAPTING FAVORITE RECIPES

With just a little rejiggering, your favorite soup, stew, or pot roast recipe can be cooked under pressure. And the recipe remake is as easy as 1-2-3. Here's what to do:

**Compare your recipe.** Look for a recipe in this book that requires a similar cut of meat (or poultry) and similar vegetables.

**Keep the proportions.** Use the same quantities of meat, vegetables, and liquid as in the book's recipe. Add seasonings, as desired.

**Approximate the time.** Use the timing of the book's recipe as a guide for estimating the cooking time for your redesigned recipe.

## ABOUT THE RECIPES

Recipes in this book are pressure-cooker easy, pressure-cooker fast, and pressure-cooker good for you. In the previous pages, I've discussed how easy and fast cooking under pressure is, but how does good for you fit in? Pressure cookers are ideal for whipping up delectable dishes, such as the ones in this book, that are packed with lean meats, luscious fruits, flavorful vegetables, and grains—all components of a balanced, healthful diet.

Described in smart-eating terms, these pressure cooker recipes are brimming with fiber—both the kind that helps keep your digestive system on track and the kind that reduces cholesterol—plus they're great sources of the health-protecting vitamins A, C and folate and the antioxidants beta-carotene (found in dark green and yellow vegetables) and lycopene (which is abundant in tomato sauce).

Is anything missing in these recipes? Yes. Tons of salt and oil, butter, hard cheeses and red meats. Studies show that small amounts of these foods won't adversely affect your health. In fact, they have nutrients, such as vitamin E, calcium, protein and sodium that you need. But consume too much of them and your weight, blood pressure, and cholesterol can climb to unhealthy levels. For a mini-lesson on what goes into a balanced diet, check out the Food Pyramid on page 14.

12

**Note:** In the food pyramid, a range of servings is given for each food group. The smaller number is for people who consume about 1,600 calories a day; the larger number is for those who consume about 2,800 calories a day.

## ABOUT THE NUTRIENT ANALYSES

The nutrient analysis that follows each recipe was calculated for a single serving. If you eat larger or smaller portions, you'll be taking in

### WHAT EQUALS A SERVING?

**BREAD, CEREAL, RICE AND PASTA GROUP:**
- 1 slice of bread
- 1 ounce of ready-to-eat cereal
- ½ cup of cooked cereal, rice or pasta

**VEGETABLE GROUP:**
- 1 cup of raw leafy vegetables
- ½ cup of other vegetables–cooked or raw–chopped
- ¾ cup of vegetable juice

**FRUIT GROUP:**
- 1 medium apple, banana, orange
- ½ cup of chopped, cooked or canned fruit
- ¾ cup of fruit juice

**MILK GROUP:**
- 1 cup of milk or yogurt
- 1½ ounces of natural cheese
- 2 ounces of processed cheese

**MEAT, POULTRY, FISH, DRY BEANS, EGGS, AND NUTS GROUP:**
- 2–3 ounces of cooked lean meat, poultry, or fish
- ½ cup of cooked dry beans or 1 egg counts as 1 ounce of lean meat. Two tablespoons of peanut butter or ⅓ cup of nuts counts as 1 ounce of meat

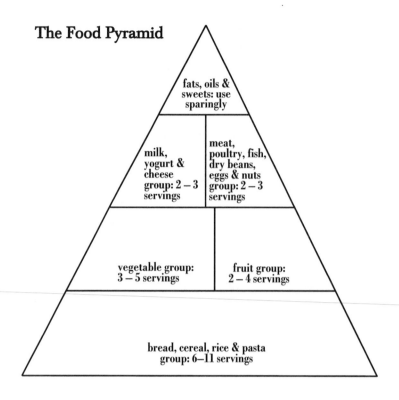

The Food Pyramid

fats, oils &
sweets: use
sparingly

milk,
yogurt &
cheese
group: 2 – 3
servings

meat,
poultry, fish,
dry beans,
eggs & nuts
group: 2 – 3
servings

vegetable group:
3 – 5 servings

fruit group:
2 – 4 servings

bread, cereal, rice & pasta
group: 6–11 servings

proportionally more or fewer calories, fat, sodium, and fiber. Whenever a recipe includes a range of ingredient amounts, say 1 to 2 teaspoons black pepper, the analysis was calculated on the smaller amount. And if a garnish or an optional ingredient is listed, that item was not calculated in the nutrient analysis.

# All Manner of Meats

## Beef Noodle Soup with Chives and Basil

*Here's a sure-fire dinner winner: Tender beef and four favorite vegetables—onions, carrots, peas, corn—simmered in a broth that's seasoned just right.*

**Makes: 4 servings**

¾ pound beef round steaks, cut into ½-inch cubes

2 cans (14 ounces each) fat-free beef broth or 4 cups homemade stock

12 baby carrots, halved lengthwise

2 onions, cut into thin wedges

8 cloves garlic, sliced

2 tablespoons balsamic vinegar

2 teaspoons Worcestershire sauce

1½ cups peas

1½ cups corn

2 cups thin noodles

2 tablespoons snipped fresh chives

¼ cup snipped fresh basil

Combine the beef, broth, carrots, onions, garlic, vinegar and Worcestershire sauce in a pressure cooker.

Place the lid on the cooker, lock it into position, and place the pressure regulator on the vent pipe if you're using a first-generation cooker. Over medium-high or high heat, bring the cooker up to pressure. Then lower the heat, adjusting it as necessary to maintain pressure (regulator should rock gently), and cook the mixture for 7 minutes.

Let the pressure drop naturally for 3 minutes; then quick-release any remaining pressure (under cold running water if you're using a first-

generation cooker). Carefully remove the pressure regulator and lid. Add the peas, corn, and noodles. Loosely cover the cooker (do not lock lid in place), and cook the soup until the vegetables are tender and the noodles are al dente. Stir in the chives and basil.

**Per serving:** 453 calories, 5.2 g fat (10% of calories), 1.6 g saturated fat, 71 mg cholesterol, 261 mg sodium, 5.9 g dietary fiber.

**Quick tip:** To serve this soup for two meals, divide it up before adding the noodles. Add the noodles to the soup right before serving. The pasta continues to absorb liquid and soften even as it's stored in the refrigerator, so the soup with noodles added doesn't keep well for a second meal.

# Beef with Red Wine Gravy

*Extra-lean eye of round adapts beautifully to pressure cooking, and a two-pound roast, including a gravy that boasts red wine, mushrooms and onions is ready to eat in a culinary flash.*

## Makes: 8 servings

olive-oil nonstick spray

2½ pound eye of round beef roast, trimmed of fat

2 onions, cut into thin wedges

4 ounces mushrooms, sliced

1 can (14 ounces) fat-free beef broth or 2 cups homemade stock

¼ cup dry red wine

4 cloves garlic, chopped

¼ cup *cold* water

2½ tablespoons instant flour

1 teaspoon browning and seasoning sauce

Coat a nonstick skillet with the spray, and warm it over medium-high heat for 1 minute. Add the beef, and cook it until it's well browned on all sides, 5 to 10 minutes. Transfer it to a pressure cooker.

In the same skillet, sauté the onions and mushrooms until they're lightly browned, about 4 minutes. Transfer the vegetables to the cooker. Add the broth, wine, and garlic.

Place the lid on the cooker, lock it into position, and place the pressure regulator on the vent pipe if you're using a first-generation cooker. Over medium-high or high heat, bring the cooker up to pressure. Then lower the heat, adjusting it as necessary to maintain pressure (regulator should rock gently), and cook the mixture for 40 minutes.

Let the pressure drop naturally for 10 minutes; then quick-release any remaining pressure (under cold running water if you're using a first-generation cooker). Carefully remove the pressure regulator and lid. Transfer the beef to a platter, leaving the broth and vegetables in the cooker; keep the beef warm.

In a small measuring cup, combine the flour, water, and seasoning sauce. Stir into the reserved broth–vegetable mixture in the cooker. Cook, uncovered, over medium heat until the onion–mushroom gravy has thickened, 4 to 5 minutes. Serve the beef sliced and topped with the gravy.

**Per serving:** 229 calories, 5.5 g fat (22% of calories), 2 g saturated fat, 78 mg cholesterol, 109 mg sodium, 0.9 g dietary fiber.

**Quick tip:** When your supermarket is temporarily out of fat-free broth, get the regular broth and de-fat it yourself. Here's how: Chill the broth in the unopened can for 1 to 2 hours. Then open the can and discard the glob of fat that's floating on the surface of the broth.

# Beer-Braised Pot Roast

*Not your run-of-the-mill pot roast: this one sports a piquant, full-bodied gravy that's seasoned with garlic, bay leaf, cinnamon, and turmeric.*

**Makes: 8 servings**

nonstick spray

2 pounds top round beef roast, trimmed of visible fat

6 onions, quartered

6 cloves garlic, pressed

8 ounces mushrooms, quartered

12 ounces nonalcoholic beer

1 bay leaf

½ cup *cold* water

¼ teaspoon ground turmeric

⅛ teaspoon ground cinnamon

2 teaspoons browning and seasoning sauce

¼ cup flour

16 ounces wide noodles

Coat a nonstick skillet with the spray, and warm it over medium-high heat for 1 minute. Add the beef, and cook it until it's brown on all sides, 5 to 10 minutes. Transfer it to a pressure cooker. Add the onions, garlic, mushrooms, beer, and bay leaf.

Place the lid on the cooker, lock it into position, and place the pressure regulator on the vent pipe if you're using a first-generation cooker. Over medium-high or high heat, bring the cooker up to pressure. Then lower the heat, adjusting it as necessary to maintain pressure (regulator should rock gently), and cook the mixture for 40 minutes.

Let pressure the drop naturally for 10 minutes; then quick-release any remaining pressure (under cold running water if you're using a first-generation cooker). Carefully remove the pressure regulator and lid. Transfer the beef to a platter, leaving the beer and vegetables in the cooker; keep the beef warm. Discard the bay leaf.

In a small measuring cup, combine the water, turmeric, cinnamon, browning sauce, and the flour. Pour it into the beer–onion mixture in the cooker. Cook uncovered over medium heat until the beer–onion gravy has thickened.

Meanwhile, cook the noodles according to package directions in a separate pot. Drain the noodles.

Slice the beef, and serve it with the beer–onion gravy and the noodles.

**Per serving:** 443 calories, 7.1 g fat (15% of calories), 2.2 g saturated fat, 53 mg cholesterol, 111 mg sodium, 3.8 g dietary fiber.

**Quick tip:** If you prefer, you can make this pot roast with regular beer or ale.

# Country Corned Beef and Cabbage

*Testers proclaimed this the most tender, tastiest corned beef they'd ever eaten. I think you'll agree.*

**Makes: 8 servings**

   2 pounds corned eye of round beef, trimmed of fat

   6 cups water

   4 bay leaves

   8 peppercorns

   ¼ cup apple cider vinegar

   8 potatoes, cut into ¾-inch pieces

   8 cups coarsely sliced cabbage

Place the beef in a pressure cooker; add the water, the bay leaves, peppercorns and vinegar.

Place the lid on the cooker, lock it into position, and place the pressure regulator on the vent pipe if you're using a first-generation cooker. Over medium-high or high heat, bring the cooker up to pressure. Then lower the heat, adjusting it as necessary to maintain pressure (regulator should rock gently), and cook the mixture for 35 minutes.

Let the pressure drop naturally for 10 minutes; then quick-release any remaining pressure (under cold running water if you're using a first-

generation cooker). Carefully remove the pressure regulator and lid. Add the potatoes.

Place the lid on the cooker, lock it into position, and place the pressure regulator on the vent pipe if you're using a first-generation cooker. Over medium-high or high heat, bring the cooker up to pressure. Then lower the heat, adjusting it as necessary to maintain pressure (regulator should rock gently), and cook the mixture for 6 minutes.

Quick-release the pressure (under cold running water if you're using a first-generation cooker). Carefully remove the pressure regulator and lid. Add the cabbage. Cook the cabbage, loosely covered (don't lock the lid into place) until it's crisp tender, 5 to 6 minutes.

Using a slotted spoon, transfer the beef, potatoes, and cabbage to a serving bowl. Discard the cooking liquid and seasonings.

**Per serving:** 214 calories, 3.9 g fat (16% of calories), 1.4 g saturated fat, 40 mg cholesterol, 628 mg sodium, 3.7 g dietary fiber.

**Quick tip:** Don't substitute brisket of corned beef for the eye of round cut; brisket has three times more fat per ounce.

# Dijon Beef with Mushrooms

*If you've been looking for a Stroganoff-style dish that's long on flavor but short on fat, this fast-to-make beef over noodles combo should fill the bill.*

## Makes: 4 servings

olive-oil nonstick spray

¾ pound beef round steak, cut into thin strips

8 ounces mushrooms, sliced

6 cloves garlic, chopped

1 cup fat-free beef broth or homemade stock

1 tablespoon red wine vinegar

1 tablespoon reduced-sodium soy sauce

10 ounces wide noodles

¾ cup nonfat sour cream

½ cup chopped roasted red peppers

2 teaspoons Dijon mustard

¼ teaspoon white pepper

Coat a nonstick skillet with the spray and warm it over medium-high heat for 1 minute. Add the beef, and sauté it until it's brown, 4 to 5 minutes. Transfer the beef to a pressure cooker.

In the same skillet, sauté the mushrooms until they're lightly browned, about 3 minutes. Transfer them to the cooker. Add the garlic, broth, vinegar, and soy sauce.

Place the lid on the cooker, lock it into position, and place the pressure regulator on the vent pipe if you're using a first-generation cooker. Over medium-high or high heat, bring the cooker up to pressure. Then lower the heat, adjusting it as necessary to maintain pressure (regulator should rock gently), and cook the mixture for 10 minutes.

Meanwhile, cook the noodles according to package directions, omitting the salt.

Let the pressure drop naturally for 5 minutes; then quick-release any remaining pressure (under cold running water if you're using a first-

generation cooker). Carefully remove the pressure regulator and lid. Stir in the roasted peppers, sour cream, mustard, and white pepper. Cook uncovered until it's hot throughout.

Drain the noodles and top them with the beef mixture.

**Per serving:** 501 calories, 5.8 g fat (11% of calories), 1.6 g saturated fat, 71 mg cholesterol, 328 mg sodium, 2.6 g dietary fiber.

**Quick tip:** For a full-bodied sauce, be sure to use a thick and substantial nonfat sour cream.

# Goulash with Mushrooms

*Cocoa is the key to the deep rich color and flavor in this no-fuss goulash, which is an adaptation of Hungarian gulyás.*

**Makes: 4 servings**

olive-oil nonstick spray

1 pound eye of round steak, cut into ½-inch cubes

6 onions, cut into thin wedges

8 ounces mushrooms, sliced

1 cup fat-free beef broth or homemade stock

1 cup crushed tomatoes

1 teaspoon cocoa

2 tablespoons paprika

⅛ teaspoon freshly ground black pepper

8 ounces wide noodles

Coat a nonstick skillet with the spray, and warm it over medium-high heat for 1 minute. Add the beef, onions, and mushrooms and cook them until they're browned, 5 to 7 minutes. Transfer them to a pressure cooker, and add the broth, tomatoes and cocoa.

Place the lid on the cooker, lock it into position, and place the pressure regulator on the vent pipe if you're using a first-generation cooker. Over medium-high or high heat, bring the cooker up to pressure. Then lower the heat, adjusting it as necessary to maintain pressure (regulator should rock gently), and cook the mixture for 8 minutes.

Let the pressure drop naturally for 6 minutes; then quick-release any remaining pressure (under cold running water if you're using a first-generation cooker). Carefully remove the pressure regulator and lid. Stir in the paprika and pepper; cook the goulash, uncovered, for 5 minutes to blend the flavors.

Meanwhile, cook the noodles according to the package directions. Drain the noodles and serve the goulash over them.

**Per serving:** 513 calories, 8.4 g fat (15% of calories), 2.6 g saturated fat, 78 mg cholesterol, 128 mg sodium, 6.3 g dietary fiber.

**Quick tip:** To brown the beef, mushrooms, and onions quickly, use a fairly hot skillet and cook small batches at a time.

# Greek-Inspired Beef Stew

*Here, cinnamon and nutmeg, two bittersweet flavors common in Greek cuisine, bring a new dimension to tomatoes and lean beef.*

**Makes: 4 servings**

nonstick spray

¾ pound beef top round steak, cut into thin ¾-inch-wide, 2-inch-long strips

4 ounces mushrooms, quartered

4 cloves garlic, chopped

1 cup fat-free beef broth or homemade stock

1 cup crushed tomatoes

1 tablespoon red wine vinegar

1 tablespoon brown sugar

2 onions, cut into wedges

1 large sweet red pepper, chopped

½ teaspoon ground cinnamon

⅛ teaspoon ground nutmeg

8 ounces medium-wide noodles

Coat a nonstick skillet with nonstick spray, and warm it over medium-high heat for 1 minute. Add the beef and mushrooms and sauté until browned, 5 to 10 minutes. Transfer the beef to a pressure cooker. Add the garlic, broth, tomatoes, vinegar, sugar, and onions.

Place the lid on the cooker, lock it into position, and place the pressure regulator on the vent pipe if you're using a first-generation cooker. Over medium-high or high heat, bring the cooker up to pressure. Then lower the heat, adjusting it as necessary to main pressure (regulator should rock gently), and cook the mixture for 5 minutes.

Meanwhile, cook the noodles in a large pot of boiling water for 3 minutes.* Drain.

Let the pressure drop naturally for 3 minutes; then quick-release any remaining pressure (under cold running water if you're using a first-generation cooker). Carefully remove the pressure regulator and lid. Stir in the red pepper, cinnamon, nutmeg, and noodles. Cook until flavors have blended and noodles are al dente, about 5 minutes.

**Per serving:** 463 calories, 5.5 g fat (11% of calories), 1.6 g saturated fat, 71 mg cholesterol, 253 mg sodium, 4.2 g dietary fiber.

**\*Quick tip:** Take care not to overcook the noodles in the boiling water. If you accidentally do, reduce the cooking time in the last step.

# Meatball and Bow Tie Pasta Soup

*Tiny meatballs made with cheese and basil fill this hearty soup with irresistible flavor.*

**Makes: 4 servings**

½ pound ground round beef

½ cup quick-cooking oats

2 tablespoons dried minced onions

2 teaspoons garlic powder

2 teaspoons dried basil

1 egg white

½ cup grated Parmesan cheese

1 can (15 ounces) whole tomatoes, cut up

3 cups fat-free beef broth or homemade stock

1 cup baby carrots, halved lengthwise

1 zucchini, halved lengthwise and sliced ½ inch thick

4 ounces bow tie pasta (farfelle)

Combine the beef, oats, 1 teaspoon of the onions, ½ teaspoon of the garlic, ½ teaspoon of the basil, egg white, and Parmesan in a bowl. Shape the mixture into 16 meatballs of 1-inch diameter. Heat a non-stick skillet over medium-high heat for 1 minute. Add the meatballs and cook them until they're brown on all sides, about 8 minutes.

Put the remaining onions, the remaining garlic, the remaining basil, the tomatoes, broth, carrots, and zucchini in a pressure cooker. Add the meatballs.

Place the lid on the cooker, lock it into position, and place the pressure regulator on the vent pipe if you're using a first-generation cooker. Over medium-high or high heat, bring the cooker up to pressure. Then lower the heat, adjusting it as necessary to maintain pressure (regulator should rock gently), and cook the mixture for 4 minutes.

Quick-release the pressure (under cold running water if you're using a first-generation cooker). Carefully remove the pressure regulator and lid. Stir in the pasta and cook the soup, uncovered, until the bow ties are al dente, 10 to 13 minutes. Divide the soup among 4 bowls and top each serving with the remaining Parmesan.

**Per serving:** 369 calories, 7.3 g fat (18% of calories), 3.1 g saturated fat, 56 mg cholesterol, 394 mg sodium, 4.9 g dietary fiber.

**Quick tip:** Be sure to form firm meatballs; loosely shaped ones may fall apart during cooking.

# Mushroom-Stuffed Beef Roll-Ups

*Here I use store-bought stuffing to minimize prep time and maximize flavor. It's a handy ingredient for those times when speed is essential.*

**Makes: 4 servings**

¾ pound beef round steaks (4 steaks)

olive-oil nonstick spray

4 ounces mushrooms, chopped

1 onion, chopped

1 celery stalk, chopped

1 cup seasoned stuffing mix

2 cups fat-free beef broth or homemade stock

1 tablespoon dry red wine

1 bay leaf

3 tablespoons *cold* water

2 tablespoons cornstarch

Freshly ground black pepper, garnish

Using a meat mallet, pound the steaks to ¼ inch thick.

Coat a nonstick skillet with the spray and warm it over medium-high heat for 1 minute. Add the mushrooms, onions, and celery, and sauté the vegetables until the mushrooms and onions are lightly browned.

In a bowl, combine the mushroom mixture with the stuffing and ½ cup of the broth. Place the mix in the center of each steak; roll each up and fasten with a toothpick. Warm the nonstick skillet again; add the roll-ups and cook them until they're browned on all sides. Transfer them to the cooker. Pour in the remaining broth and the wine. Add the bay leaf.

Place the lid on the cooker, lock it into position, and place the pressure regulator on the vent pipe if you're using a first-generation cooker. Over medium-high or high heat, bring the cooker up to pressure. Then lower the heat, adjusting it as necessary to maintain pressure (regulator should rock gently), and cook the mixture for 10 minutes.

Let the pressure drop naturally for 5 minutes; then quick-release any remaining pressure (under cold running water if you're using a first-generation cooker). Carefully remove the pressure regulator and lid. Transfer the beef to a platter, leaving the broth in the cooker; keep the beef warm. Discard the bay leaf.

Combine the cornstarch and cold water in a small measuring cup. Pour the mixture into the broth in the cooker. Cook, uncovered, over medium heat until the gravy is thickened, about 2 minutes. Place a roll-up with gravy on each of 4 plates. Sprinkle the pepper over each serving.

**Per serving:** 243 calories, 4.7 g fat (18% of calories), 1.5 g saturated fat, 72 mg cholesterol, 296 mg sodium, 1.2 g dietary fiber.

**Quick tip:** Chop the mushrooms, onions, and celery fairly fine. Small pieces make it easier to roll up the stuffing and beef.

# Old-Fashioned Pot Roast with Vegetables

*I must admit, this home-style meal with plenty of meat, potatoes, and gravy is one of my favorites.*

## Makes: 8 servings

nonstick spray

2 pounds eye of round beef roast, trimmed of visible fat

1 can (14 ounces) fat-free beef broth or 2 cups homemade stock

1 tablespoon red wine vinegar

4 potatoes, peeled and halved

4 carrots, peeled and halved

1 celery stalk, quartered

2 onions, quartered

4 ounces mushroom caps

¼ cup *cold* water

2 teaspoons browning and seasoning sauce

¼ cup flour

Coat a nonstick skillet with the spray and warm it over medium-high heat for 1 minute. Add the beef, and cook it until it's brown on all sides, 5 to 10 minutes. Place a rack or trivet in a pressure cooker. Transfer the beef to the cooker and add the broth, vinegar, potatoes, carrots, celery, onions, and mushrooms.

Cover the cooker, lock the lid into position, and place the pressure regulator on the vent pipe if you're using a first-generation cooker. Over medium-high or high heat, bring the cooker up to pressure. Then lower the heat, adjusting it as necessary to maintain pressure (regulator should rock gently), and cook the mixture for 45 minutes.

Let the pressure drop naturally for 15 minutes; then quick-release any remaining pressure (under cold running water if you're using a first-generation cooker). Carefully remove the pressure regulator and lid. Transfer the beef and vegetables to a platter, leaving the liquid in the cooker; keep them warm. Remove the rack.

Combine the water, brown gravy flavoring, and flour in a small measuring cup. Pour into the liquid in the cooker. Cook, uncovered, over medium heat until the gravy is thickened, about 15 minutes.

Slice the beef and serve with the vegetables and gravy.

**Per serving:** 308 calories, 5.6 g fat (16% of calories), 2 g saturated fat, 78 mg cholesterol, 132 mg sodium, 3 g dietary fiber.

**Quick tip:** Always combine flour with a cold liquid before using it to thicken a hot liquid; otherwise, it'll form lumps that are nearly impossible to get rid of.

# Sauerbraten

*Sauerbraten usually simmers for three to four hours, but under pressure it's ready to eat in just one hour. This recipe features the same pungent flavors found in traditional recipes.*

**Makes: 4 servings**

- 1 onion, cut into wedges
- 4 whole cloves
- 1 teaspoon mixed peppercorns (sometimes called pepper melange; it includes whole allspice)
- 1 tablespoon pickling spice
- 1 cup dry red wine
- 1 cup fat-free beef broth or homemade stock
- 1 pound bottom round beef roast, trimmed of fat
- ½ cup fine gingersnap crumbs
- ½ cup nonfat sour cream

In a medium-size bowl, combine the onions, cloves, peppercorns, pickling spice, wine, and broth. Add the beef and let it marinate in the refrigerator for at least 24 hours, turning it once or twice. Transfer the beef and marinade to a pressure cooker.

Place the lid on the cooker, lock it into position, and place the pressure regulator on the vent pipe if you're using a first-generation cooker. Over medium-high or high heat, bring the cooker up to pressure. Then lower the heat, adjusting it as necessary to maintain pressure (regulator should rock gently), and cook the mixture for 45 minutes.

Let the pressure drop naturally for 10 minutes; then quick-release any remaining pressure (under cold running water if you're using a first-generation cooker). Carefully remove the pressure regulator and lid. Transfer the beef to a platter, leaving the broth and spices in the cooker.

Pour the broth mixture through a large strainer into a 2-quart saucepan. Discard the spices and onions. Stir the gingersnaps into the broth; cook the mixture, uncovered, over medium heat until the gravy has thickened. Stir in the sour cream.

Slice the meat and serve it topped with the gravy.

**Per serving:** 376 calories, 8.5 g fat (21% of calories), 2.4 g saturated fat, 88 mg cholesterol, 297 mg sodium, 1.5 g dietary fiber.

**Quick tip:** Substitute whole black peppercorns if you can't find the mixed variety.

# Spaghetti Sauce with Meatballs

*This Italian-style tomato sauce and the ultra-lean meatballs (they're made with ground round and ground turkey breast) come together in about 30 minutes.*

**Makes: 4 servings**

¼ pound ground round beef

¼ pound ground turkey breast

½ cup quick-cooking oats

3 tablespoons minced dried onions

2 tablespoons dried parsley

2 teaspoons garlic powder

2 teaspoons Italian herb seasoning

¾ teaspoon crushed red pepper flakes

1 egg white

2 teaspoons grated Parmesan cheese

1 can (28 ounces) crushed tomatoes

1 cup fat-free beef broth or homemade stock

½ teaspoon allspice

In a large bowl, combine the beef, turkey, oats, 1 teaspoon onions, 2 teaspoons parsley, ½ teaspoon garlic, ½ teaspoon herb seasoning, ¼ teaspoon red pepper flakes, the egg white, and 2 teaspoons Parmesan cheese. Form the meat mixture into 16 meatballs. Warm a nonstick skillet over medium-high heat, and cook the meatballs until they're browned on all sides, 5 to 10 minutes.

Pour the tomatoes and broth into a pressure cooker. Stir in the all-spice, the remaining onions, remaining parsley, remaining garlic, remaining red pepper flakes, and remaining herb seasoning. Add the meatballs.

Place the lid on the cooker, lock it into position, and place the pressure regulator on the vent pipe if you're using a first-generation cooker. Over medium-high or high heat, bring the cooker up to pressure. Then lower the heat, adjusting it as necessary to maintain pressure (regulator should rock gently), and cook the mixture for 4 minutes.

Let the pressure drop naturally for 2 minutes; then quick-release any

remaining pressure (under cold running water if you're using a first-generation cooker). Carefully remove the pressure regulator and lid.

**Per serving:** 234 calories, 4.3 g fat (15% of calories), 1.2 g saturated fat, 48 mg cholesterol, 132 mg sodium, 6.3 g dietary fiber.

**Quick tip:** Use garlic powder, not garlic salt, when you want intense flavor and no added sodium. Garlic powder has nary a milligram of sodium in a teaspoon; in the same serving size, garlic salt has between 1,000 and 2,000 milligrams of sodium, depending on the brand.

# Swedish Meatballs

*That classic of the holiday buffet, Swedish meatballs, with their singular allspice and nutmeg seasoning, makes for a delightfully quick and delicious dinner.*

**Makes: 4 servings**

1 cup fat-free beef broth or homemade stock

¼ pound ground round beef

¼ pound ground pork

½ cup quick-cooking oats

1 egg white

2 tablespoons dried minced onions

1 tablespoon dried parsley

¾ teaspoon allspice

½ teaspoon ground nutmeg

½ teaspoon Worcestershire sauce

8 ounces wide noodles

½ cup nonfat sour cream

Pour the broth into a pressure cooker.

Combine the beef, pork, oats, egg white, onions, parsley, allspice, nutmeg, and Worcestershire sauce in a large bowl. Form the mixture into 16 walnut-size balls. Heat a nonstick skillet over medium-high heat for 1 minute. Add the meatballs and cook them until they're browned on all sides, 5 to 8 minutes. Transfer them to the cooker.

Place the lid on the cooker, lock it into position, and place the pressure regulator on the vent pipe if you're using a first-generation cooker. Over medium-high or high heat, bring the cooker up to pressure. Then lower the heat, adjusting it as necessary to maintain pressure (regulator should rock gently), and cook the mixture for 5 minutes.

Let the pressure drop naturally for 7 minutes; then quick-release any remaining pressure (under cold running water if you're using a first-generation cooker). Carefully remove the pressure regulator and lid. Transfer the meatballs to a platter, leaving the broth in the cooker.

Meanwhile, cook the noodles according to package directions, omitting any salt.

Stir the sour cream into the broth and cook over medium heat, uncovered, until the gravy is hot (but do not let it boil).

Drain the noodles and serve them topped with the meatballs and gravy.

**Per serving:** 416 calories, 6.9 g fat (15% of calories), 2.2 g saturated fat, 49 mg cholesterol, 145 mg sodium, 2.8 g dietary fiber.

**Quick tip:** For maximum flavor, the meatballs should be well-browned before they're cooked in the pressure cooker.

# Ukrainian-Style Borscht

*Just 10 fresh ingredients—not the usual 20 to 30—make up this traditional-tasting beet soup.*

**Makes: 4 servings**

   ½ cup dried small white beans, soaked in hot water at least 1 hour

water

   2 cans (14 ounces each) fat-free beef broth or 4 cups homemade stock

   ¾ pound eye of round steak, cut into ½-inch cubes

   1 onion, cut into thin wedges

   4 beets, peeled and cut into ½-inch cubes

   1 tablespoon red wine vinegar

   2 cups coarsely sliced cabbage

   ¼ teaspoon freshly ground black pepper

   ¼ cup snipped fresh dill

nonfat sour cream, garnish

Drain the beans and place them in a pressure cooker; cover them with an inch of water.

Place the lid on the cooker, lock it into position, and place the pressure regulator on the vent pipe if you're using a first-generation cooker. Over medium-high or high heat, bring the cooker up to pressure. Then lower the heat, adjusting it as necessary to maintain pressure (regulator should rock gently), and cook the mixture for 3 minutes.

Quick-release the pressure (under cold running water if you're using a first-generation cooker). Carefully remove the pressure regulator and lid. Drain the beans and return them to the cooker. Add the broth and beef.

Place the lid on the cooker, lock it into position, and place the pressure regulator on the vent pipe if you're using a first-generation cooker. Over medium-high or high heat, bring the cooker up to pressure. Then lower the heat, adjusting it as necessary to maintain pressure (regulator should rock gently), and cook for 5 minutes.

Quick-release the pressure (under cold running water if you're using a first-generation cooker). Carefully remove the pressure regulator and lid. Add the onions, beets, and red wine vinegar.

Place the lid on the cooker, lock it into position, and place the pressure regulator on the vent pipe if you're using a first-generation cooker. Over medium-high or high heat, bring the cooker up to pressure. Then lower the heat, adjusting it as necessary to maintain pressure (regulator should rock gently), and cook the mixture for 5 minutes.

Quick-release the pressure (under cold running water if you're using a first-generation cooker). Carefully remove the pressure regulator and lid. Add the cabbage, pepper and dill and cook the soup, loosely covered (don't lock the lid into place), until the cabbage is tender, about 5 minutes.

Divide the soup among 4 bowls; garnish each serving with a tablespoon of the sour cream.

**Per serving:** 317 calories, 4.6 g fat (13% of calories), 1.6 g saturated fat, 59 mg cholesterol, 268 mg sodium, 4.6 g dietary fiber.

**Quick tips:** To substitute canned beets for the fresh ones, simply add the beets along with the cabbage and dill. And if you can't find any fresh dill, use 2 tablespoons dill weed instead.

# Bacon and Beans

*Have a craving for that sweet-savory, bean-laden dish that bakes for hours and hours? When you're in a rush, this 20-minute version is sure to please. Now's a good time to give it a shot.*

**Makes: 4 servings**

1 cup dried small white beans, soaked in hot water at least 1 hour
water
1 onion, chopped
1 cup (6 ounces) chopped cooked Canadian bacon
1 cup fat-free beef broth or homemade stock
¼ cup tomato paste
2 tablespoons brown sugar
1 teaspoon mustard powder
½ teaspoon chili powder

Drain the beans and place them in a pressure cooker; cover them with an inch of water.

Place the lid on the cooker, lock it into position, and place the pressure regulator on the vent pipe if you're using a first-generation cooker. Over medium-high or high heat, bring the cooker up to pressure. Then lower the heat, adjusting it as necessary to maintain pressure (regulator should rock gently), and cook the mixture for 9 minutes.

Quick-release the pressure (under cold running water if you're using a first-generation cooker). Carefully remove the pressure regulator and lid. Drain the beans and return them to the cooker. Add the onions, bacon, broth, tomato paste, sugar, mustard, and chili powder.

Place the lid on the cooker, lock it into position, and place the pressure regulator on the vent pipe if you're using a first-generation cooker. Over medium-high or high heat, bring the cooker up to pressure. Then lower the heat, adjusting it as necessary to maintain pressure (regulator should rock gently), and cook the mixture for 2 minutes.

Let the pressure drop naturally for 10 minutes; then quick-release any remaining pressure (under cold running water if you're using a first-

generation cooker). Carefully remove the pressure regulator and lid.

**Per serving:** 290 calories, 3.3 g fat (10% of calories), 0.8 g saturated fat, 19 mg cholesterol, 528 mg sodium, 1.4 g dietary fiber.

**Quick tip:** You can use either light or dark brown sugar in this recipe. Don't pack the sugar when measuring it.

# Black Bean and Ham Soup

*This lively soup gets its dusky flavor from hickory smoke concentrate, which is available in most supermarkets.*

## Makes: 6 servings

¾ cup dried black beans, soaked in hot water for at least 1 hour

water

nonstick spray

1½ cups (¾ pound) cubed lean, reduced-sodium ham

1 onion, chopped

3 cans (14 ounces each) fat-free beef broth or 6 cups homemade
   stock

4 plum tomatoes, chopped

1 cup cooked rice

3 carrots, thinly sliced

6 cloves garlic, chopped

1½ teaspoons thyme

1 bay leaf

1 to 2 teaspoons Louisiana hot-pepper sauce

1 teaspoon hickory smoke flavoring

Drain the beans and place them in a pressure cooker; cover them with an inch of water.

Place the lid on the cooker, lock it into position, and place the pressure regulator on the vent pipe if you're using a first-generation cooker. Over medium-high or high heat, bring the cooker up to pressure. Then lower the heat, adjusting it as necessary to maintain pressure (regulator should rock gently), and cook the mixture for 7 minutes.

Meanwhile, coat a nonstick skillet with the spray, and warm it over medium-high heat for 1 minute. Add the ham and onions to the skillet, and cook them until they're lightly browned, about 5 minutes.

Quick-release the pressure (under cold running water if you're using a first-generation cooker). Carefully remove the pressure regulator and lid. Drain the beans and return them to the cooker.

Add the ham, onions, broth, tomatoes, rice, and carrots. Stir in the garlic, thyme, and bay leaf.

Place the lid on the cooker, lock it into position, and place the pressure regulator on the vent pipe if you're using a first-generation cooker. Over medium-high or high heat, bring the cooker up to pressure. Then lower the heat, adjusting it as necessary to maintain pressure (regulator should rock gently), and cook the mixture for 1 minute.

Quick-release the pressure (under cold running water if you're using a first-generation cooker). Carefully remove the pressure regulator and lid. Stir in the hot-pepper sauce and smoke flavoring.

**Per serving:** 235 calories, 2.7 g fat (10% of calories), 0.8 g saturated fat, 19 mg cholesterol, 623 mg sodium, 6.2 g dietary fiber.

**Quick tip:** Some hot-pepper sauces, such as Tabasco, are scorchingly hot. If you're using one of these varieties, add the sauce by the drops, not the teaspoonful.

# Lamb–Vegetable Soup

*Kale, a crisp, vitamin-A-packed green that's plentiful in the fall, perks up this casual soup.*

**Makes: 4 servings**

olive-oil nonstick spray

¾ pound lean lamb, cut into ¾-inch cubes

1 can (14 ounces) stewed tomatoes

1 cup cooked barley

2½ cups fat-free beef broth or homemade stock

6 cloves garlic, chopped

2 onions, chopped

4 carrots, sliced

2 potatoes, cut into ½-inch cubes

2 teaspoons dried sage

1 cup torn kale

¼ teaspoon freshly ground black pepper

Coat a nonstick skillet with the oil spray and warm it over medium-high heat for 1 minute. Add the lamb, and cook it until it's browned, 4 to 5 minutes. Transfer the lamb to a pressure cooker. Add the tomatoes, barley, garlic, onion, carrots, potatoes, and sage.

Place the lid on the cooker, lock it into position, and place the pressure regulator on the vent pipe if you're using a first-generation cooker. Over medium-high or high heat, bring the cooker up to pressure. Then lower the heat, adjusting it as necessary to maintain pressure (regulator should rock gently), and cook the mixture for 12 minutes.

Let the pressure drop naturally for 5 minutes; then quick-release any remaining pressure (under cold running water if you're using a first-generation cooker). Carefully remove the pressure regulator and lid. Stir in the kale and pepper, and cook the soup, uncovered, until the kale has wilted, 1 to 3 minutes.

**Per serving:** 429 calories, 6.9 g fat (14% of calories), 2.2 g saturated fat, 74 mg cholesterol, 439 mg sodium, 10.6 g dietary fiber.

**Quick tip:** Here's a quick-and-easy way to remove garlic's tenacious skin: Wrap the clove in a rubber jar-gripper and, applying a little pressure, roll the clove on the countertop. Zap, the garlic's skinless!

# Cider Pork Roast

*In this recipe, sweet apple cider spiced with peppercorns and mustard makes a perfect braising liquid for pork tenderloin.*

**Makes: 4 servings**

butter-flavored nonstick spray

1 pound pork tenderloin

2 cups apple cider or juice

1 can (14 ounces) fat-free chicken broth or 2 cups homemade stock

2 tablespoons minced dried onions

1 tablespoon mixed peppercorns (also called peppercorn melange; it includes allspice)

2 teaspoons mustard seeds

2 bay leaves

1 teaspoon celery seeds

4 tablespoons *cold* water

3 tablespoons cornstarch

Coat a nonstick skillet with the spray, and warm it over medium-high heat for 1 minute. Add the pork, and cook it until browned on all sides, 5 to 8 minutes. Transfer the pork to a pressure cooker. Add the cider, broth, onion, peppercorns, mustard, bay leaves, and celery seeds.

Place the lid on the cooker, lock it into position, and place the pressure regulator on the vent pipe if you're using a first-generation cooker. Over medium-high or high heat, bring the cooker up to pressure. Then lower the heat, adjusting it as necessary to maintain pressure (regulator should rock gently), and cook the mixture for 35 minutes.

Let the pressure drop naturally for 15 minutes; then quick-release any remaining pressure (under cold running water if you're using a first-generation cooker). Carefully remove the pressure regulator and lid.

Transfer the pork to a platter, leaving the cider and seasonings in the cooker; keep the pork warm.

Pour the cider–broth mixture through a large strainer into a 2-quart saucepan. Discard the seasonings. Combine the cold water and corn-starch in a cup; stir the cornstarch mixture into the cider–broth mixture, and cook the gravy, uncovered, until it's hot and slightly thickened.

**Per serving:** 300 calories, 6.1 g fat (19% of calories), 1.9 g saturated fat, 89 mg cholesterol, 140 mg sodium, 1 g dietary fiber.

**Quick tip:** You can substitute mustard powder and ground celery seed for the whole seeds, if you wish. Just be aware that the gravy may be murky looking and the flavor slightly different.

# Cumin-Seasoned Pork with Mushrooms

*A popular Tex-Mex flavor trio—cumin, jalapeño peppers, and cilantro— enlivens these lean pork chops, which are served over noodles.*

**Makes: 4 servings**

butter-flavored nonstick spray

¾ pound center-cut pork chops (4 chops)

6 ounces mushroom caps

1 can (14 ounces) fat-free beef broth or 2 cups homemade stock

8 cloves garlic, chopped

2 tablespoons sherry

2 jalapeño peppers, seeded and chopped

2 teaspoons cumin seeds

8 ounces wide noodles

¼ cup *cold* water

4 tablespoons instant flour

2 tablespoons snipped fresh cilantro

Coat a nonstick skillet with the spray and warm it over medium-high heat for 1 minute. Add the pork and cook it until it's browned on both sides, 5 to 10 minutes. Transfer the pork to a pressure cooker.

Add the mushrooms to the skillet and sauté them until they're golden, 4 to 5 minutes. Transfer the mushrooms to the cooker, and add the broth, garlic, sherry, peppers, and cumin.

Place the lid on the cooker, lock it into position, and place the pressure regulator on the vent pipe if you're using a first-generation cooker. Over medium-high or high heat, bring the cooker up to pressure. Then lower the heat, adjusting it as necessary to maintain pressure (regulator should rock gently), and cook the mixture for 8 minutes.

Meanwhile, cook the noodles according to package directions, omitting salt.

Let the pressure on the cooker drop naturally for 2 minutes; then quick-release any remaining pressure (under cold running water if you're using a first-generation cooker). Carefully remove the pressure regulator and lid. Transfer the pork to a platter, leaving the liquid and mushrooms in the cooker.

Combine the cold water and flour in a small cup. Pour the flour mixture into the broth–mushroom mixture, and cook, uncovered, over medium heat until it's slightly thickened, 2 to 4 minutes. Stir in the cilantro.

Drain the noodles. Serve the pork over the noodles.

**Per serving:** 454 calories, 8.3 g fat (17% of calories), 2.7 g saturated fat, 70 mg cholesterol, 128 mg sodium, 2.4 g dietary fiber.

**Quick tip:** Wear gloves when seeding and mincing jalapeño peppers. Capsaicin, the substance responsible for the peppers' heat, can sting your fingertips.

# Gingered Pork Over Rice

*Here's a 20-minute dish that sports the signature tastes of an Asian stir-fry: salty (soy sauce), spicy (gingerroot), and sweet (apple juice).*

**Makes: 4 servings**

3 cups fat-free beef broth or homemade stock

1 cup wild pecan rice or white long-grain rice

butter-flavored nonstick spray

1 pound center-cut pork chops, cut into ¾-inch cubes

3 tablespoons apple juice

1 tablespoon reduced-sodium soy sauce

6 cloves garlic, chopped

1 tablespoon minced gingerroot

2 tablespoons cornstarch

4 tablespoons *cold* water

Snipped fresh parsley, garnish

In a 3-quart pot, bring 2 cups of the beef broth to a boil. Stir in the rice and cook it until the rice is tender and the liquid has been absorbed, about 20 minutes.

Meanwhile, coat a nonstick skillet with the spray and warm it over medium-high heat for 1 minute. Add the pork, and cook it until it's brown, 3 to 5 minutes. Transfer it to a pressure cooker. Add the remaining broth, the juice, soy sauce, garlic and gingerroot.

Place the lid on the cooker, lock it into position, and place the pressure regulator on the vent pipe if you're using a first-generation cooker. Over medium-high or high heat, bring the cooker up to pressure. Then lower the heat, adjusting it as necessary to maintain pressure (regulator should rock gently), and cook the mixture for 6 minutes.

Let the pressure drop naturally for 5 minutes; then quick-release any remaining pressure (under cold running water if you're using a first-generation cooker). Carefully remove the pressure regulator and lid.

Combine the cold water and cornstarch in a small measuring cup. Pour into the pork mixture. Cook, uncovered, over medium heat until the liquid is slightly thickened, 1 to 3 minutes. Serve the pork and gravy over the rice. Garnish with the parsley.

**Per serving:** 417 calories, 9.6 g fat (21% of calories), 3.4 g saturated fat, 93 mg cholesterol, 343 mg sodium, 2.7 g dietary fiber.

**Quick tip:** Stash gingerroot in a cool, dry place or freeze it. To freeze the root, pare off the papery skin and place the root in a plastic bag.

# Jamaican Jerk Pork

*This trendy entrée gets its flavorful, hot zing from a rub with eight spices, including pungent cloves and nippy peppers.*

## Makes: 4 servings

2 cups fat-free beef broth or homemade stock

2 teaspoons dried minced onions

1 teaspoon dried thyme

1 teaspoon garlic powder

1 teaspoon crushed red pepper flakes

¼ teaspoon cinnamon

¼ teaspoon powdered ginger

¼ teaspoon allspice

⅛ teaspoon cloves

1 pound pork tenderloin

3 tablespoons *cold* water

2 tablespoons cornstarch

Pour the broth into a pressure cooker. Place a rack or trivet in the bottom of the cooker.

In a small bowl, combine the onions, thyme, garlic, red pepper flakes, cinnamon, ginger, allspice and cloves. Rub the spice mixture into all sides of the pork. Place the pork on the rack in the cooker.

Place the lid on the cooker, lock it into position, and place the pressure regulator on the vent pipe if you're using a first-generation cooker. Over medium-high or high heat, bring the cooker up to pressure. Then lower the heat, adjusting it as necessary to maintain pressure (regulator should rock gently), and cook the mixture for 35 minutes.

Let the pressure drop naturally for 15 minutes; then quick-release any

remaining pressure (under cold running water if you're using a first-generation cooker). Carefully remove the pressure regulator and lid. Transfer the pork to a platter, leaving the broth in the cooker; keep the pork warm.

In a small cup whisk together the cold water and cornstarch. Stir the cornstarch into the broth, and cook the gravy, uncovered, until it's slightly thickened and hot. Slice the pork and serve it with the gravy.

**Per serving:** 224 calories, 5.6 g fat (23% of calories), 1.9 g saturated fat, 89 mg cholesterol, 147 mg sodium, 0.4 g dietary fiber.

**Quick tip:** Some supermarkets carry jerk seasoning. If yours does, give the prepared combo a try.

# Pork Chops and Onions with Lime Slices

*No matter how often I serve this super-simple dish, it's always a big hit. Sometimes, I vary it with lemon instead of lime and rice instead of potatoes. (Cook the rice separately.)*

**Makes: 4 servings**

nonstick spray

4 center-cut loin pork chops (about 1 pound), trimmed of visible fat

¾ cup fat-free chicken broth or homemade stock

2 cups crushed tomatoes

1 onion, cut into 4 thick slices

1 lime, cut into 4 thick slices

1 teaspoon ground thyme

4 potatoes, peeled

½ teaspoon lemon pepper

½ sweet yellow pepper, cut into 4 thin rings

sprigs of flat-leaf parsley, garnish

Coat a nonstick skillet with the spray and warm it over medium-high heat for 1 minute. Add the pork chops and cook until they are brown on both sides, which will take about 3 minutes.

Pour the tomatoes and broth into a pressure cooker. Place the pork chops in a single layer in the cooker (it's okay if they overlay). Top each with a slice each of the onion and lime. Add the thyme. Place the potatoes on top.

Place the lid on the cooker, lock it into position, and place the pressure regulator on the vent pipe if you're using a first-generation cooker. Over medium-high or high heat, bring the cooker up to pressure. Then lower the heat, adjusting it as necessary to maintain pressure (regulator should rock gently), and cook the mixture for 8 minutes.

Let the pressure drop naturally for 10 minutes; then quick-release any remaining pressure (under cold running water if you're using a first-generation cooker). Carefully remove the pressure regulator and lid. Stir in the lemon pepper.

Serve the chops and potatoes topped with the tomatoes and pepper rings. Garnish with the parsley.

**Per serving:** 384 calories, 6.8 g fat (16% of calories), 2.3 g saturated fat, 61 mg cholesterol, 99 mg sodium, 7.7 g dietary fiber.

**Quick tips:** If you can't find lemon pepper, substitute freshly ground black pepper in this recipe. If you are using rice instead of potatoes, cook the rice in a separate pot, following the package directions. Start cooking the rice when you start the chops.

# Pork Chops in Dill Sauce

*Dill's a delicate herb that marries well with lean pork; stir it into this and other recipes toward the end of cooking to get its full lemony essence.*

**Makes: 4 servings**

> 1 can (14 ounces) fat-free beef broth or 2 cups homemade stock
>
> nonstick spray
>
> 4 center cut loin pork chops (about 1 pound), trimmed of visible fat
>
> 1 onion, chopped
>
> 1 bay leaf
>
> 4 potatoes, peeled and halved
>
> 1/4 teaspoon freshly ground black pepper
>
> 1 tablespoon snipped fresh dill or 1 teaspoon dried
>
> 2 tablespoons cornstarch

Pour 1½ cups broth into the pressure cooker. Coat a nonstick skillet with spray and warm it over medium-high heat for 1 minute. Add the pork chops, and cook them until they're brown on both sides, 4 to 6 minutes. Transfer to the cooker. Add the onions, bay leaf, and potatoes.

Place the lid on the cooker, lock it into position, place the pressure regulator on the vent pipe if you're using a first-generation cooker. Over medium-high or high heat, bring the cooker up to pressure. Then lower the heat, adjusting it as necessary to maintain pressure (regulator should rock gently), and cook the mixture for 8 minutes.

Let the pressure drop naturally, 15 to 20 minutes. Carefully remove the lid. Transfer the pork and potatoes to a platter, leaving the broth and onions; keep the meat and vegetables hot.

Whisk together the pepper, dill, cornstarch, and remaining broth. Pour the mixture into the broth–onion mixture; heat, uncovered, until the sauce is hot. Serve the pork and potatoes topped with the onion–dill sauce.

**Per serving:** 371 calories, 6.4 g fat (16% of calories), 2.3 g saturated fat, 61 mg cholesterol, 124 mg sodium, 6.2 g dietary fiber.

**Quick tip:** Avoid cooking the cornstarch-thickened sauce too long or stirring it too vigorously, or it will thin.

# Veal Chops with Olives and Capers

*Here's an enticing entrée that's sophisticated enough for a company dinner yet simple enough for an everyday supper, thanks to a special blend of bacon, capers, and olives.*

## Makes: 4 servings

nonstick spray

2 pounds veal shoulder chops

1 cup fat-free beef broth or homemade stock

4 cloves garlic, chopped

1 small onion, chopped

1 tablespoon finely chopped Canadian bacon

1 tablespoon minced black olives

2 teaspoons capers, rinsed

3 tablespoons *cold* water

2 tablespoons cornstarch

Coat a nonstick skillet with the spray and warm it over medium-high heat for 1 minute. Add the veal, and cook the chops until they're brown on both sides. Transfer the veal to a pressure cooker. Add the broth, garlic, onions, and bacon.

Place the lid on the cooker, lock it into position, and place the pressure regulator on the vent pipe if you're using a first-generation cooker. Over medium-high or high heat, bring the cooker up to pressure. Then lower the heat, adjusting it as necessary to maintain pressure (regulator should rock gently), and cook the mixture for 10 minutes.

Let the pressure drop naturally for 10 minutes; then quick-release any remaining pressure (under cold running water if you're using a first-generation cooker). Carefully remove the pressure regulator and lid. Transfer the veal to a platter, leaving the broth–bacon mixture. Keep the veal warm.

In a cup, whisk together the cold water and the cornstarch. Stir the olives and capers into the broth–bacon mixture; stir in the cornstarch mixture. Cook the sauce, uncovered, until it's slightly thickened, 1 to 3 minutes. Serve the veal topped with the olive–caper sauce.

**Per serving:** 268 calories, 8.7 g fat (30% of calories), 3.2 g saturated fat, 150 mg cholesterol, 292 mg sodium, 0.5 g dietary fiber.

**Quick tips:** You can substitute green olives for the black ones in this recipe; just be aware that the green variety has more sodium. And remember to rinse capers to remove excess sodium before using them.

# Veal Piccata

*In this fast version of piccata, a classic dish hailing from Italy, dry white wine and shallots complement the traditional ingredients of veal, lemon, and parsley.*

## Makes: 4 servings

¾ cup fat-free chicken broth or homemade stock

¼ cup dry white wine

4 shallots, sliced

olive-oil nonstick spray

1 pound veal cutlets

juice of ½ lemon

¼ teaspoon freshly ground black pepper

1 tablespoon snipped fresh parsley

Place the broth, wine, and shallots in a pressure cooker.

Coat a nonstick skillet with the spray and warm it over medium-high heat for 1 minute. Add the veal and cook it until it's browned on both sides, about 5 minutes. Transfer the veal to the cooker.

Place the lid on the cooker, lock it into position, and place the pressure regulator on the vent pipe if you're using a first-generation cooker. Over medium-high or high heat, bring the cooker up to pressure. Then lower the heat, adjusting it as necessary to maintain pressure (regulator should rock gently), and cook the mixture for 3 minutes.

Let the pressure drop naturally for 3 minutes; then quick-release any remaining pressure (under cold running water if you're using a first-

generation cooker). Carefully remove the pressure regulator and lid. Transfer the veal to a platter, leaving the broth and shallots in the cooker; keep the veal warm. Pour the lemon juice and pepper into the broth. Serve the veal topped with the shallots, broth, and parsley.

**Per serving:** 166 calories, 4 g fat (22% of calories), 1.6 g saturated fat, 87 mg cholesterol, 92 mg sodium, 0.6 g dietary fiber.

**Quick tip:** Use freshly ground black pepper whenever you can; it has more zip and zing than the preground variety.

# Plenty of Poultry

## Chicken Curry

*There are curry dishes. And there are great curry dishes. This one ranks with the best. And it's extra-easy to make, too.*

**Makes: 4 servings**

> 1 cup brown rice
>
> nonstick spray
>
> 1 pound boneless, skinless chicken breast, cut into ¾-inch pieces
>
> 4 large onions, cut into thin wedges
>
> 1¼ cups water
>
> 4 cloves garlic, chopped
>
> 1 teaspoon peanut oil
>
> 1 tablespoon reduced-sodium soy sauce
>
> 1 teaspoon chili powder
>
> 1 teaspoon curry powder
>
> ¼ teaspoon ground turmeric
>
> 1 teaspoon ground ginger
>
> 2 tablespoons snipped fresh parsley

In a 3-quart saucepan, cook the rice according to package directions, omitting salt and butter.

Meanwhile, coat a nonstick skillet with the spray and warm it over medium-high heat for 1 minute. Add the chicken and onions, and sauté the mixture until the chicken is lightly browned, about 5 minutes. Transfer the chicken and onions to a pressure cooker. Add the water, garlic, oil, and soy sauce; stir in the chili powder, curry, turmeric, and ginger.

Place the lid on the cooker, lock it into position, and place the pressure regulator on the vent pipe if you're using a first-generation cooker. Over medium-high or high heat, bring the cooker up to pressure. Then lower the heat, adjusting it as necessary to maintain pressure (regulator should rock gently), and cook the mixture for 4 minutes.

Let the pressure drop naturally for 4 minutes; then quick-release any remaining pressure (under cold running water if you're using a first-generation cooker). Carefully remove the pressure regulator and lid.

Stir in parsley and serve over the hot rice.

**Per serving:** 454 calories, 6 g fat (12% of calories), 1.5 g saturated fat, 95 mg cholesterol, 252 mg sodium, 4.9 g dietary fiber.

**Quick tip:** For less sodium in a full-flavored soy sauce, use reduced-sodium soy sauce. It has 50% less sodium than the regular variety, but the taste is much the same.

# Chicken Paprikás with Caraway

*Heavily seasoned with paprika (the ground pods of a special sweet pepper variety), chicken paprikás commands a favored spot on Hungarian menus. This spirited version is pressure cooker fast.*

**Makes: 4 servings**

- butter-flavored nonstick spray
- 4 skinless, boneless chicken breast halves (1 pound)
- ¾ cup fat-free chicken broth or homemade stock
- ¼ cup sherry
- 4 cloves garlic, chopped
- 8 ounces wide noodles
- 2 tablespoons paprika
- 2 teaspoons caraway seeds
- ¾ cup nonfat sour cream

Coat a nonstick skillet with the spray and warm it over medium-high heat for 1 minute. Add the chicken, and cook it until it's brown on both sides, 10 to 12 minutes. Transfer the chicken to a pressure cooker. Add the broth, sherry, and garlic.

Place the lid on the cooker, lock it into position, and place the pressure regulator on the vent pipe if you're using a first-generation cooker. Over medium-high or high heat, bring the cooker up to pressure. Then lower the heat, adjusting it as necessary to maintain pressure (regulator should rock gently), and cook the mixture for 6 minutes.

Meanwhile, cook the noodles according to package directions.

Let the pressure drop naturally for 4 minutes; then quick-release any remaining pressure (under cold running water if you're using a first-generation cooker). Carefully remove the pressure regulator and lid. Transfer the chicken to a platter, leaving the liquid. Stir the paprika, caraway, and sour cream into the liquid.

Drain the noodles. Top them with the chicken and sauce.

**Per serving:** 536 calories, 5.7 g (10% of calories), 1.4 g saturated fat, 95 mg cholesterol, 182 mg sodium, 2.4 g dietary fiber.

**Quick tip:** For a smooth sour cream sauce, heat the mixture until the sauce is hot, but don't let it boil.

# Chicken Picadillo

*Translate picadillo from Spanish to English and what have you got? Hash. Here, cubed chicken replaces the usual ground pork, and the hash is rolled up in a warm tortilla. Serve this speedy supper with salsa–medium or hot, depending on your palate's preference–and nonfat sour cream, if desired.*

## Makes: 4 servings

1 pound boneless, skinless chicken breasts, cut
 into ½-inch cubes

2 large onions, chopped

8 cloves garlic, minced

1 can (15 ounces) diced tomatoes

½ cup raisins

1 sweet red pepper, finely chopped

1 mild chili pepper, seeded and finely chopped

1 stick cinnamon

3 tablespoons instant flour

¼ teaspoon crushed red pepper flakes

6 black olives, sliced, optional

8 corn tortillas, warmed

Warm a nonstick skillet for 30 seconds over medium-high heat. Place the chicken, onions, and garlic in the skillet, and cook them until the chicken is lightly browned, about 5 minutes. Transfer the mixture to a pressure cooker. Stir in the tomatoes, raisins, sweet peppers, chili peppers, and cinnamon.

Place the lid on the cooker, lock it into position, and place the pressure regulator on the vent pipe if you're using a first-generation cooker. Over medium-high or high heat, bring the cooker up to pressure. Then lower the heat, adjusting it as necessary to maintain pressure (regulator should rock gently), and cook the mixture for 5 minutes.

Let the pressure drop naturally for 5 minutes; then quick-release any remaining pressure (under cold running water if you're using a first-generation cooker). Carefully remove the pressure regulator and lid.

Discard the cinnamon. Stir in the flour, red pepper flakes, and olives. Heat until the mixture has thickened, 2 to 5 minutes.

Spoon hash down center of each tortilla. Roll up and serve.

**Per serving:** 474 calories, 6.8 g fat (12% of calories), 1.5 g saturated fat, 95 mg cholesterol, 239 mg sodium, 8 g dietary fiber.

**Quick tip:** To heat tortillas, wrap them in foil and bake in a 350° oven for 5 to 7 minutes.

# Chicken with Spicy Noodles

*Treat your taste buds to hot pepper zest and peanut crunch with this Szechuan-inspired dinner.*

**Makes: 4 servings**

1 pound boneless skinless chicken breast, cut into ¾-inch pieces

1 cup fat-free chicken broth or homemade stock

4 cloves garlic, minced

1 sweet red pepper, cut into thin strips

1¼ cups sliced scallions

1 tablespoon minced gingerroot

½ teaspoon crushed red pepper flakes

2 tablespoons reduced-fat peanut butter

1 tablespoon reduced-sodium soy sauce

10 ounces angel-hair pasta

2 tablespoons chopped unsalted peanuts

2 tablespoons snipped fresh parsley

Combine the chicken, broth, and garlic in a pressure cooker. Place the lid on the cooker, lock it into position, and place the pressure regulator on the vent pipe if you're using a first-generation cooker. Over medium-high or high heat, bring the cooker up to pressure. Then lower the heat, adjusting it as necessary to maintain pressure (regulator should rock gently), and cook the mixture for 6 minutes.

Quick-release the pressure (under cold running water if you're using a

first-generation cooker). Stir in the sweet pepper, scallions, gingerroot, and pepper flakes. Loosely cover the cooker (do not lock the lid in place), and cook for 5 minutes. Combine the peanut butter and soy sauce, and stir the mixture into the chicken–vegetable mixture. Heat, uncovered, for 3 minutes.

Meanwhile, cook the noodles according to package directions. Drain the noodles. Serve the chicken over the noodles and top with the peanuts and parsley.

**Per serving:** 511 calories, 9.6 g fat (17% of calories), 2 g saturated fat, 71 mg cholesterol, 265 mg sodium, 3.3 g dietary fiber.

**Quick tip:** Can't find any angel-hair pasta? Pick up some vermicelli or spaghettini instead.

# Lime Chicken Rice Soup

*Anytime is a good time to enjoy this soul-satisfying soup, the one that's said to perk you up when you're feeling down with a cold or the flu. In this easy version you'll find a new twist—a twist of lime.*

**Makes: 4 servings**

2 cans (14 ounces each) fat-free chicken broth or 3½ cups home-made stock

1 celery stalk, sliced diagonally into ½-inch pieces

2 carrots, sliced into ½-inch pieces

1 onion, chopped

1 bay leaf

½ pound boneless, skinless chicken breast, cut into ½-inch pieces

1 cup cooked long-grain rice

juice of 1 lime

1 teaspoon grated lime peel

½ teaspoon freshly ground black pepper

1 teaspoon snipped fresh lemon thyme or ¼ teaspoon dried

Combine the broth, celery, carrots, onions, bay leaf, and chicken in a pressure cooker.

Place the lid on the cooker, lock it into position, and place the pressure regulator on the vent pipe if you're using a first-generation cooker. Over medium-high or high heat, bring the cooker up to pressure. Then lower the heat, adjusting it as necessary to maintain pressure (regulator should rock gently), and cook the mixture for 5 minutes.

Let the pressure drop naturally for 5 minutes; then quick-release any remaining pressure (under cold running water if you're using a first-generation cooker). Carefully remove the pressure regulator and lid. Discard the bay leaf. Stir in the rice, lime juice and peel, black pepper, and thyme. Heat the mixture for 3 minutes, uncovered, to blend flavors and heat the rice.

**Per serving:** 207 calories, 2.3 g fat (10% of calories), 1 g saturated fat, 48 mg cholesterol, 205 mg sodium, 2.3 g dietary fiber.

**Quick tip:** Don't have cooked rice on hand, and don't want to cook up a batch for just 1 cup? Here's how to change the recipe to use raw rice: Add an extra cup of water with the chicken broth. Then after quick-releasing the pressure, stir in ½ cup rice along with the lime juice and peel, black pepper, and thyme. Loosely cover the cooker (do not lock lid in place) and cook until the rice is tender, 10 to 15 minutes.

# Mandarin Chicken

*Sweet and colorful, oranges—the mandarin variety, to be specific—brighten chicken and noodles in this Asian-influenced main dish. And did you know that mandarin oranges and tangerines are close cousins?*

**Makes: 4 servings**

- ¾ pound boneless, skinless chicken breasts
- 1 tablespoon balsamic vinegar
- 1 can (14 ounces) fat-free chicken broth or 2 cups homemade stock
- 1 onion, cut into thin wedges
- 1 teaspoon dried tarragon
- 1 can (11 ounces) mandarin oranges, drained
- 1 tablespoon honey
- 1 tablespoon reduced-sodium soy sauce
- 4 tablespoons cornstarch
- 8 ounces Chinese wheat noodles
- ¼ cup cold water
- freshly ground black pepper, garnish

Combine chicken, vinegar, broth, and onions in a pressure cooker.

Place the lid on the cooker, lock it into position, and place the pressure regulator on the vent pipe if you're using a first-generation cooker. Over medium-high or high heat, bring the cooker up to pressure. Then lower the heat, adjusting it as necessary to maintain pressure (regulator should rock gently), and cook the mixture for 5 minutes.

Let the pressure drop naturally for 10 minutes; then quick-release any remaining pressure (under cold running water if you're using a first-generation cooker). Carefully remove the lid, and transfer the chicken to a platter, leaving the broth in the cooker. Keep the chicken warm. Stir in the tarragon, oranges, honey, and soy sauce.

Meanwhile, cook the noodles according to package directions.

Combine the cornstarch and water. Stir into the broth mixture in the cooker, and cook, uncovered, over medium heat until the sauce has thickened.

Drain the noodles. Serve the chicken and sauce over the hot noodles. Garnish with the pepper.

**Per serving:** 464 calories, 4.6 g fat (9% of calories), 0.9 g saturated fat, 71 mg cholesterol, 317 mg sodium, 3.9 g dietary fiber.

**Quick tip:** To cut an onion into thin wedges, halve a peeled onion from stem to root end, then slice the halves vertically into wedges.

# Moroccan-Inspired Chicken Stew

*By themselves, there's nothing unique about cardamom, lemon, ginger, dates, cinnamon, and chickpeas. But combine them and they provide the special flavors of a North African cuisine.*

**Makes: 4 servings**

   3 cups fat-free chicken broth, or homemade stock

   1 tablespoon grated lemon peel

   juice of 1 lemon

   ¼ teaspoon cardamom

   ¼ teaspoon ground ginger

   ¼ teaspoon ground cinnamon

   ½ cup chopped, pitted dates

   1 can (15 ounces) chickpeas, rinsed and drained

   1 teaspoon olive oil

   ¾ pound boneless chicken breasts, cut into 1-inch cubes

   1 large onion, cut into wedges

   1 cup couscous

   1 teaspoon red pepper flakes

Combine 1 cup of the broth, the lemon peel and juice, cardamom, ginger, cinnamon, dates, and chickpeas in a pressure cooker.

Place the olive oil in a nonstick skillet, and warm it over medium-high heat for 1 minute. Add the chicken and onions, and sauté them until they're lightly browned, 5 to 7 minutes. Transfer them to the cooker.

Place the lid on the cooker, lock it into position, and place the pressure regulator on the vent pipe if you're using a first-generation cooker. Over medium-high or high heat, bring the cooker up to pressure. Then lower the heat, adjusting it as necessary to maintain pressure (regulator should rock gently), and cook the mixture for 5 minutes.

Meanwhile, in the same skillet used earlier, bring the remaining broth to a boil. Stir in the couscous. Cover the skillet, remove it from the heat, and let it sit for 5 minutes.

Let the pressure in the cooker drop naturally for 3 minutes; then quick-release any remaining pressure (under cold running water if you're using a first-generation cooker). Carefully remove the pressure regulator and lid. Stir in the red pepper flakes. Serve the stew over the couscous.

**Per serving:** 482 calories, 5.8 g fat (11% of calories), 1.4 g saturated fat, 95 mg cholesterol, 247 mg sodium, 5.4 g dietary fiber.

**Quick tip:** To get the most from a lemon, grate the peel first, being careful to remove the colored part only (the white pith tastes bitter). Next, microwave the lemon on medium for 25 seconds and roll it, applying a little pressure, on a countertop. Halve the lemon and squeeze.

# Pineapple Chicken with Asian Vegetables

*Asian cuisines often use luscious fruits, like pineapple or oranges, to offset the pungent bite of spices such as ginger and hot peppers. Pineapple is featured in this enticing dish. Serve with these condiments: duck sauce and Chinese garlic chili sauce.*

**Makes: 4 servings**

1 pound boneless, skinless chicken breasts, cut into ¾-inch pieces

1 can (20 ounces) pineapple chunks, drained, juice reserved

1 cup long-grain rice

¾ cup sliced scallions

1 tablespoon minced gingerroot

1 tablespoon dry sherry

1 tablespoon reduced-sodium soy sauce

1 can (8 ounces) water chestnuts, drained and rinsed

½ teaspoon crushed red pepper flakes

2 tablespoons cornstarch

¼ cup *cold* water

Combine chicken and reserved pineapple juice in a pressure cooker. The juice should measure 1 cup; if it doesn't, add enough water to bring it up to the cup mark.

Meanwhile, in a 3-quart pot, cook the rice according to package directions, omitting the salt and butter.

Place the lid on the cooker, lock it into position, and place the pressure regulator on the vent pipe if you're using a first-generation cooker. Over medium-high or high heat, bring the cooker up to pressure. Then lower the heat, adjusting it as necessary to maintain pressure (regulator should rock gently), and cook the mixture for 10 minutes.

Quick-release the pressure (under cold running water if you're using a first-generation cooker). Carefully remove the pressure regulator and lid. Stir in the scallions, gingerroot, sherry, soy sauce, water chestnuts, and red pepper flakes. Cover the cooker loosely, and cook the mixture 5 minutes to blend flavors.

Combine the cornstarch and water. Stir the cornstarch mixture into the pineapple-chicken mixture, and cook, uncovered, until the liquid is thickened, 1 to 2 minutes. Serve the pineapple chicken over the rice.

**Per serving:** 501 calories, 4.5 g fat (8% of calories), 1.2 g saturated fat, 95 mg cholesterol, 246 mg sodium, 3.5 g dietary fiber.

# Pollo Cacciatore

*Cacciatore lovers take note: This hunter-style stew is full to the brim with tender chicken, garlic, tomatoes, red wine, mushrooms and other ingredients that make Mediterranean foods so decidedly magnifico. Serve over mafalda or rotini, and top everything with snipped fresh Italian parsley and sliced green olives.*

## Makes: 4 servings

¾ pound boneless, skinless chicken breasts, cut into 8 pieces

⅓ cup whole wheat flour

4 teaspoons olive oil

2 large scallions, sliced

4 cloves garlic, chopped

1 cup quartered small white mushroom caps

1 sweet green pepper, sliced into thin slices

1 can (28 ounces) plum tomatoes, cut up, with liquid

½ cup light Italian red wine

¼ teaspoon ground celery seed

½ teaspoon Italian herb seasoning

¼ teaspoon freshly ground black pepper

Coat the chicken on all sides with the flour. Heat 2 teaspoons of the olive oil in a nonstick skillet, and warm it over medium-high heat for 1 minute. Add the chicken, and cook the pieces until they're lightly browned on both sides, about 5 minutes. Transfer the chicken to a pressure cooker.

In the same skillet, heat the remaining olive oil and sauté the scallions, garlic, pepper and mushrooms until the onions are translucent, about 3 minutes. Transfer the vegetables to the cooker and add the tomatoes with liquid and the wine.

Place the lid on the cooker, lock it into position, and place the pressure regulator on the vent pipe if you're using a first-generation cooker. Over medium-high or high heat, bring the cooker up to pressure. Then lower the heat, adjusting it as necessary to maintain pressure (regulator should rock gently), and cook the mixture for 6 minutes.

Let the pressure drop naturally for 5 minutes; then quick-release any remaining pressure (under cold running water if you're using a first-generation cooker). Carefully remove the pressure regulator and lid. Stir in the celery seed, Italian seasoning and black pepper.

**Per serving:** 291 calories, 8.5 g fat (26% of calories), 1.6 g saturated fat, 71 mg cholesterol, 84 mg sodium, 4.1 g dietary fiber.

**Quick tip:** Though you can use a domestic Italian-style wine in this recipe, you might want to try an imported Valpolicella or Bardolino. Neither is expensive, and the taste is dry and pleasant.

# Shrimp, Chicken, and Sausage Jambalaya

*This Creole specialty is bursting with the marvelous flavors of tomatoes, onions, and peppers, not to mention shrimp, chicken, and sausage.*

**Makes: 4 servings**

1⅛ cups rice

½ pound boneless, skinless chicken breast, cut into ½-inch pieces

¼ pound medium shrimp, peeled and deveined

¼ pound turkey kielbasa sausage, halved and thinly sliced

1 onion, cut into thin wedges

1 can (14 ounces) stewed tomatoes

6 cloves garlic, chopped

3 bay leaves

1 sweet green pepper, chopped

1½ cups sliced okra

1 teaspoon Louisiana hot sauce

In a 3-quart saucepan, cook the rice according to package directions, omitting salt and butter.

Meanwhile, combine the chicken, shrimp, sausage, onions, tomatoes, bay leaves, and garlic in a pressure cooker.

Place the lid on the cooker, lock it into position, and place the pressure regulator on the vent pipe if you're using a first-generation cooker. Over medium-high or high heat, bring the cooker up to pressure. Then lower the heat, adjusting it as necessary to maintain pressure (regulator should rock gently), and cook the mixture for 4 minutes.

Let pressure drop naturally for 2 minutes; then quick-release any remaining pressure (under cold running water if you're using a first-generation cooker). Carefully remove the pressure regulator and lid. Discard the bay leaves. Stir in the green pepper, okra, and hot sauce. Loosely cover the cooker and cook the jambalaya until the okra is done and the flavors are blended, 5 to 8 minutes. Serve over the hot rice.

**Per serving:** 425 calories, 5.3 g fat (11% of calories), 1.5 g saturated fat, 108 mg cholesterol, 560 mg sodium, 3.1 g dietary fiber.

**Quick tip:** Use a mild brand of hot sauce or add the sauce a drop at a time. See "quick tip" with Black Bean and Ham Soup.

# Alphabet Turkey Soup

*Are you up for some good eating and writing your name in pasta at the same time? This family-favorite soup has the ingredients—turkey, corn, roasted peppers, and tiny alphabet pasta—that the young and young-at-heart love.*

## Makes: 4 servings

olive-oil nonstick spray

1 pound turkey slices (or cutlets), cut into ½-inch cubes

4 cups fat-free turkey or chicken broth or homemade stock

1 onion, chopped

2 carrots, diced

⅛ teaspoon turmeric

1 cup (2 ounces) alphabet pasta

1 cup peas

1 cup corn

¼ cup roasted red peppers

1 teaspoon thyme

¼ teaspoon freshly ground black pepper

Coat a nonstick skillet with the spray and warm it over medium-high heat for 1 minute. Add the turkey, and cook it until the pieces are lightly browned, 4 to 5 minutes. Transfer the turkey to a pressure cooker. Add the stock, onions, carrots, and turmeric.

Place the lid on the cooker, lock it into position, and place the pressure regulator on the vent pipe if you're using a first-generation cooker. Over medium-high or high heat, bring the cooker up to pressure. Then lower the heat, adjusting it as necessary to maintain pressure (regulator should rock gently), and cook the mixture for 5 minutes.

Let the pressure drop naturally for 5 minutes; then quick-release any

remaining pressure (under cold running water if you're using a first-generation cooker). Carefully remove the pressure regulator and lid.

Stir in the pasta and cook, uncovered, for 10 minutes. Stir in the peas, corn, red peppers, thyme, and black pepper. Cook until the vegetables are tender and the pasta is al dente, about 4 minutes.

**Per serving:** 376 calories, 1.6 g fat (4% of calories), 0.4 g saturated fat, 94 mg cholesterol, 283 mg sodium, 5.5 g dietary fiber.

**Quick tip:** In a hurry? In this recipe, canned roasted red peppers work just as well as fresh peppers that you roast yourself.

# Barbecued Turkey Sandwiches

*For an informal supper that's ready in no time, a robust and not-too-spicy sandwich like this one is in order.*

**Makes: 4 sandwiches**

  olive-oil nonstick spray
  1 pound boneless, skinless turkey breast strips
  1 can (15 ounces) diced tomatoes
  1 cup fat-free chicken broth or homemade stock
  1 onion, chopped
  3/4 teaspoon chili powder
  2 tablespoons brown sugar
  1 tablespoon spicy brown mustard
  1 teaspoon Worcestershire sauce
  2 tablespoons cider vinegar
  3/4 cup chopped roasted red peppers
  4 tablespoons instant flour
  4 whole wheat Kaiser rolls

Coat a nonstick skillet with the spray, and warm it over medium-high heat for 1 minute. Add the turkey and cook it for 4 minutes. Transfer it to a pressure cooker. Add the tomatoes, broth, onions, chili, sugar, mustard, Worcestershire, and vinegar.

Place the lid on the cooker, lock it into position, and place the pressure regulator on the vent pipe if you're using a first-generation cooker. Over medium-high or high heat, bring the cooker up to pressure. Then lower the heat, adjusting it as necessary to maintain pressure (regulator should rock gently), and cook the mixture for 4 minutes.

Let the pressure drop naturally for 5 minutes; then quick-release any remaining pressure (under cold running water if you're using a first-generation cooker). Stir in the peppers and the flour. Cook, uncovered, until the flavors are blended and the mixture is slightly thickened, 3 to 5 minutes.

**Per sandwich:** 332 calories, 3 g fat (8% of calories), 0.6 g saturated fat, 94 mg cholesterol, 319 mg sodium, 2.1 g dietary fiber.

**Quick tip:** If your supermarket doesn't carry instant flour, a specially formulated flour that dissolves without lumping, use all-purpose flour instead. To keep it from lumping, stir it into ¼ cup cold water before adding it to the hot liquid.

# Mexican-Inspired Turkey with Pinto Beans

*Mole, a dark, spicy Mexican sauce, was the inspiration for the season-ing combination in this stick-to-your-ribs main dish.*

**Makes: 4 servings**

½ cup pinto beans, soaked in hot water at least 1 hour

water

2 onions, cut into wedges

1 can (14 ounces) diced tomatoes

1 cup fat-free beef broth or homemade stock

6 cloves garlic, chopped

2 tablespoons chili powder

1 teaspoon ground cumin

1 teaspoon cocoa

½ teaspoon oregano

olive-oil nonstick spray

¾ pound turkey breast slices, cut into thin 1-inch long strips

2 tablespoons snipped fresh cilantro

Drain the beans and place them in a pressure cooker; cover them with an inch of water.

Place the lid on the cooker, lock it into position, and place the pressure regulator on the vent pipe if you're using a first-generation cooker. Over medium-high or high heat, bring the cooker up to pressure. Then lower the heat, adjusting it as necessary to maintain pressure (regulator should rock gently), and cook the beans for 8 minutes.

Quick-release the pressure (under cold running water if you're using a first-generation cooker). Carefully remove the pressure regulator and lid. Drain the beans and return them to the cooker. Stir in the onions, tomatoes, broth, garlic, chili powder, cumin, cocoa, and oregano.

Coat a nonstick skillet with the spray and warm it over medium-high heat for 1 minute. Add the turkey, and cook it until it's lightly browned, 3 to 5 minutes. Transfer it to the cooker.

Place the lid on the cooker, lock it into position, and place the pressure regulator on the vent pipe if you're using a first-generation cooker. Over medium-high or high heat, bring the cooker up to pressure. Then lower the heat, adjusting it as necessary to maintain pressure (regulator should rock gently), and cook for 6 minutes.

Quick-release the pressure (under cold running water if you're using a first-generation cooker). Carefully remove the pressure regulator and lid. Divide the stew among 4 plates; top each serving with cilantro.

**Per serving:** 259 calories, 1.7 g fat (6% of calories), 0.3 g saturated fat, 71 mg cholesterol, 114 mg sodium, 8.8 g dietary fiber.

**Quick tip:** In a pinch, fresh parsley can be substituted for cilantro, which is sometimes called fresh coriander.

# Rustic Turkey Stew

*When your taste buds call for lean turkey and vegetables in a creamy thyme sauce, this stew could be the answer.*

## Makes: 4 servings

olive-oil nonstick spray

1 pound turkey breast, cut into ¾-inch cubes

2 onions, cut into wedges

1 can (14 ounces) fat-free chicken broth or 2 cups homemade stock

3 red potatoes, cut into ¾-inch cubes

3 carrots, cut into ¾-inch slices

2 cups frozen or fresh cut green beans

½ sweet red pepper, chopped

2 teaspoons dried thyme leaves

⅛ teaspoon white pepper

½ cup powdered milk

2 tablespoons instant flour

Coat a nonstick skillet with the spray and warm it over medium-high heat for 1 minute. Add the turkey and onions, and cook them until they're lightly brown, 4 to 6 minutes. Transfer the turkey–onion mixture to a pressure cooker.

Add the broth, potatoes, carrots, green beans, sweet pepper, thyme, and white pepper to the cooker.

Place the lid on the cooker, lock it into position, and place the pressure regulator on the vent pipe if you're using a first-generation cooker. Over medium-high or high heat, bring the cooker up to pressure. Then lower the heat, adjusting it as necessary to maintain pressure (regulator should rock gently), and cook the mixture for 6 minutes.

Let the pressure drop naturally for 5 minutes; then quick-release any remaining pressure (under cold running water if you're using a first-generation cooker). Carefully remove the pressure regulator and lid. Stir in the milk and flour. Cook, uncovered, until the mixture has thickened, about 5 minutes.

**Per serving:** 360 calories, 1.3 g fat (3% of calories), 0.4 g saturated fat, 96 mg cholesterol, 210 mg sodium, 7 g dietary fiber.

**Quick tip:** To use fresh thyme in this recipe, use 1 tablespoonful and stir it in after pressure cooking the mixture.

# Sausage, Turkey and Shrimp Stew

*Here's a fabulous fish and fowl feast for family and friends, and it cooks in 20 minutes or less.*

**Makes: 4 servings**

1 cup wild pecan rice

½ pound turkey kielbasa, halved and thinly sliced

¼ pound turkey cutlets, cut into ¾-inch pieces

6 ounces peeled and deveined medium shrimp, halved

3 large onions, cut into wedges

2 large red sweet peppers, chopped

8 cloves garlic, chopped

1 tablespoon Italian herb seasoning

1 tablespoon paprika

1 can (14 ounces) stewed tomatoes

1 cup fat-free chicken broth or homemade stock

1 tablespoon chopped black olives

In a 3-quart saucepan, cook the rice according to package directions, omitting salt and butter.

Sauté the sausage and turkey in a nonstick skillet until the turkey is lightly browned. Transfer the mixture to a pressure cooker. Add the shrimp, onions, peppers, garlic, herb seasoning, paprika, tomatoes, and broth.

Place the lid on the cooker, lock it into position, and place the pressure regulator on the vent pipe if you're using a first-generation cooker. Over medium-high or high heat, bring the cooker up to pressure. Then lower the heat, adjusting it as necessary to maintain pressure (regulator should rock gently), and cook the mixture for 5 minutes.

Let the pressure drop naturally for 5 minutes; then quick-release any remaining pressure (under cold running water if you're using a first-generation cooker). Carefully remove the pressure regulator and lid. Serve over the rice and top with the olives.

**Per serving:** 448 calories, 7.1 g fat (14% of calories), 2 g saturated fat, 124 mg cholesterol, 665 mg sodium, 4.2 g dietary fiber.

**Quick tip:** You can substitute 1 teaspoon each dried basil, dried oregano, and dried thyme for the Italian herb seasoning.

# Sausage and Pepper Soup

*Made from a concoction that includes pork, fennel, and hot peppers, Italian sausage takes center stage in this differently delicious meal.*

**Makes: 4 servings**

½ pound hot Italian turkey sausage

2 onions, chopped

2 cans (14 ounces each) fat-free chicken broth or homemade stock

1 can (15 ounces) diced tomatoes

6 cloves garlic, chopped

1 yellow squash, halved lengthwise and sliced ½ inch thick

1 large sweet green pepper, cut into thin 2-inch-long strips

1½ teaspoons Italian herb seasoning

½ teaspoon red pepper flakes

1½ cups rotini

grated Parmesan cheese, garnish

Cook the sausage and onions in a nonstick skillet until the sausage is lightly browned. Halve the sausage lengthwise and slice it ½ inch thick. Place the sausage and onions into a pressure cooker. Add the broth, tomatoes, and garlic to the cooker.

Place the lid on the cooker, lock it into position, and place the pressure regulator on the vent pipe if you're using a first-generation cooker. Over medium-high or high heat, bring the cooker up to pressure. Then lower the heat, adjusting it as necessary to maintain pressure (regulator should rock gently), and cook the mixture for 5 minutes.

Quick-release the pressure (under cold running water if you're using a first-generation cooker). Carefully remove the pressure regulator and lid. Stir in the squash, sweet pepper, herb seasoning, and red pepper.

Add the rotini, and cook the soup, uncovered, until the rotini are al dente, 12 to 15 minutes. Garnish each serving with the Parmesan.

**Per serving:** 450 calories, 7 g fat (13% of calories), 1.8 g saturated fat, 35 mg cholesterol, 674 mg sodium, 9.9 g dietary fiber.

**Quick tip:** If the supermarket is out of canned diced tomatoes, substitute canned whole tomatoes and cut them up yourself.

# Stuffed Cabbage Leaves

*An easy-to-make bread and ground turkey stuffing gives these attractive cabbage roll-ups plenty of palate appeal.*

## Makes: 4 servings

4 large cabbage leaves

1 cup water

1½ cups stuffing mix

1 can (14 ounces) fat-free chicken broth or homemade stock

olive-oil nonstick spray

1 pound ground turkey breast

1 onion, chopped

½ teaspoon dried basil

½ teaspoon dried sage

¼ teaspoon freshly ground black pepper

½ cup canned diced tomatoes

1 teaspoon dried savory

Place the cabbage and water into a pressure cooker.

Place the lid on the cooker, lock it into position, and place the pressure regulator on the vent pipe if you're using a first-generation cooker. Over medium-high or high heat, bring the cooker up to pressure. Immediately remove the cooker from the heat.

Meanwhile, in a bowl, combine the stuffing and ¾ cup of the broth.

Quick-release the pressure (under cold running water if you're using a

first-generation cooker). Carefully remove the pressure regulator and lid. Remove the cabbage and spread the leaves on paper towels. Discard the water.

Coat a nonstick skillet with the spray and warm it over medium-high heat for 1 minute. Add the turkey and onions, and sauté the mixture until the turkey is no longer pink, 5 to 7 minutes, stirring occasionally to crumble the turkey. Stir in the basil, sage, and black pepper; add the stuffing mixture. Divide the turkey-stuffing mixture among the cabbage leaves. Fold in the sides of each leaf and roll it up. Place the cabbage rolls, seam-side down, in the pressure cooker. Pour in the remaining broth.

Place the lid on the cooker, lock it into position, and place the pressure regulator on the vent pipe if you're using a first-generation cooker. Over medium-high or high heat, bring the cooker up to pressure. Then lower the heat, adjusting it as necessary to maintain pressure (regulator should rock gently), and cook the mixture for 1 minute.

Quick-release the pressure (under cold running water if you're using a first-generation cooker). Carefully remove the pressure regulator and lid. Transfer the cabbage rolls to a serving dish, leaving the broth; keep the rolls warm. Stir the tomatoes and savory into the broth and heat the mixture until it's hot throughout. Serve over the cabbage rolls.

**Per serving:** 274 calories, 1.8 g fat (6% of calories), 0.3 g saturated fat, 94 mg cholesterol, 551 mg sodium, 0.8 g dietary fiber.

**Quick tip:** To keep this recipe ultra-lean, be sure to get ground turkey breast. Regular ground turkey (sometimes marked "lean ground turkey") usually contains dark meat plus some skin and fat and has a fat level rivaling that of ground beef.

# Turkey, Carrot and Apple Stew

*At the end of a busy day, beat the clock with this sensational dish that mixes sweet (apples and raisins) with spicy (curry and hot pepper sauce).*

## Makes: 4 servings

olive-oil nonstick spray

1¼ pounds boneless, skinless turkey breast slices, cut into strips

2 onions, cut into wedges

1 can (14 ounce) fat-free chicken broth or 2 cups homemade stock

1 celery stalk, sliced ¼ inch thick

½ cup raisins

6 carrots, sliced ½ inch thick

1 teaspoon brown sugar

½ teaspoon curry powder

⅛ teaspoon ground turmeric

1½ cups chopped McIntosh apples

2 tablespoons cornstarch

3 tablespoons *cold* water

1 teaspoon Louisiana hot sauce, or to taste

Coat a nonstick skillet with the spray and warm it over medium-high heat for 1 minute. Add the turkey and onions, and cook them until they're browned, 4 to 6 minutes. Transfer them to a pressure cooker, and add the broth, celery, raisins, carrots, brown sugar, curry powder, and turmeric.

Place the lid on the cooker, lock it into position, and place the pressure regulator on the vent pipe if you're using a first-generation cooker. Over medium-high or high heat, bring the cooker up to pressure. Then lower the heat, adjusting it as necessary to maintain pressure (regulator should rock gently), and cook the mixture for 5 minutes.

Let the pressure drop naturally for 2 minutes; then quick-release any remaining pressure (under cold running water if you're using a first-generation cooker). Carefully remove the pressure regulator and lid. Stir in the apples. Loosely cover the cooker (don't seal it), and cook the mixture for 1 to 2 minutes to soften the apples.

In a small cup, whisk together the cold water and cornstarch. Stir the cornstarch mixture into the turkey mixture, and cook the stew over medium heat until the sauce has thickened, 1 to 2 minutes.

**Per serving:** 574 calories, 1.6 g fat (2% of calories), 0.4 g saturated fat, 118 mg cholesterol, 222 mg sodium, 6.2 g dietary fiber.

**Quick tip:** When McIntosh apples aren't in season, use almost any other popular apple: Cortland, Empire, Golden Delicious, Granny Smith, Rome Beauty, Winesap.

# Turkey with Cranberry–Currant Sauce

*The popular flavors of cranberries, oranges, and turkey team up in this delectable entrée.*

## Makes: 4 servings

1 cup fat-free chicken broth or homemade stock

1 onion, chopped

½ cup currants or raisins

nonstick spray

1 pound turkey breast fillets

4 potatoes, peeled and quartered

½ cup jellied cranberry sauce

1 teaspoon grated orange peel

1 orange, with sections cut into ½-inch pieces

Pour the broth into a pressure cooker. Add the onions and currants.

Coat a nonstick skillet with the spray, and warm it over medium-high heat for 1 minutes. Add the turkey, and sauté the fillets until they're browned on both sides, about 5 minutes. Transfer them to the cooker. Add the potatoes.

Place the lid on the cooker, lock it into position, and place the pressure regulator on the vent pipe if you're using a first-generation cooker. Over medium-high or high heat, bring the cooker up to pressure. Then lower the heat, adjusting it as necessary to maintain pressure (regulator should rock gently), and cook the mixture for 8 minutes.

Let the pressure drop naturally for 2 minutes; then quick-release any remaining pressure (under cold running water if you're using a first-generation cooker). Carefully remove the pressure regulator and lid. Transfer the turkey and potatoes to a platter, leaving the broth and onions; keep the turkey and potatoes hot.

Add the cranberry sauce, orange peel, and orange sections to the broth and onion mixture. Cook the mixture until the cranberries have melted and the sauce is slightly thickened, 3 to 5 minutes. Serve the sauce over the turkey fillets.

**Per serving:** 413 calories, 1.1 g fat (2% of calories), 0.3 g saturated fat, 94 mg cholesterol, 119 mg sodium, 5.7 g dietary fiber.

**Quick tip:** Turkey breast fillets are sometimes difficult to find. If you can't locate any, use breast slices instead.

# Turkey with Creole Seasoning

*Spice rubs are hot! Use this one to add character to a succulent steamed turkey breast. The rub gets its fire from black, white, and red peppers.*

## Makes: 4 servings

2¼ cups fat-free turkey or chicken broth or homemade stock

2 teaspoons paprika

1½ teaspoons garlic powder

1½ teaspoons freshly ground black pepper

1½ teaspoons dried minced onions

1½ teaspoons crushed red pepper flakes

¾ teaspoon dried thyme

¾ teaspoon white pepper

1 pound boneless, skinless turkey breast

3 tablespoons *cold* water

2 tablespoons cornstarch

½ teaspoon browning and seasoning sauce

Pour the stock into a pressure cooker. Place a rack or trivet in the cooker.

In a small bowl, combine the paprika, garlic, black pepper, onions, red pepper, thyme, and white pepper. Rub the seasonings on all sides of the turkey breast. Place the turkey on the rack in the cooker.

Place the lid on the cooker, lock it into position, and place the pressure regulator on the vent pipe if you're using a first-generation cooker. Over medium-high or high heat, bring the cooker up to pressure. Then lower the heat, adjusting it as necessary to maintain pressure (regulator should rock gently), and cook the mixture for 25 minutes.

Let the pressure drop naturally for 15 minutes; then quick-release any remaining pressure (under cold running water if you're using a first-generation cooker). Carefully remove the pressure regulator and lid. Transfer the turkey to a platter, leaving the broth in the cooker; keep the turkey warm.

In a small cup, combine the water, cornstarch, and browning sauce. Pour the cornstarch mixture into the broth and cook the gravy, uncovered, until it's slightly thickened, about 3 minutes. Slice the turkey and serve it with the gravy.

**Per serving:** 203 calories, 1.1 g fat (5% of calories), 0.3 g saturated fat, 94 mg cholesterol, 162 mg sodium, 0.7 g dietary fiber.

**Quick tip:** For more intense flavor, chill the seasoned breast for an hour before cooking it.

# Turkey in White Wine Sauce

*Use any pleasant-tasting dry white wine in this sauce. So long as the wine is dry, not sweet, it'll impart the right delightful nuance.*

**Makes: 4 servings**

½ cup dry white wine

¾ cup fat-free chicken broth or homemade stock

nonstick spray

4 slices Canadian-style bacon

1 package (10 ounces) pearl onions

4 ounces small mushroom caps

4 boneless skinless turkey breast slices (about 1 pound)

1 tablespoon cornstarch

¼ teaspoon freshly ground black pepper

½ teaspoon dried thyme leaves

⅛ teaspoon ground celery seed

8 ounces broad noodles

Pour the wine and ½ cup broth into a pressure cooker.

Coat a nonstick skillet with the spray, and warm it over medium-high heat for 1 minute. Add the bacon and brown it on both sides, about 3 minutes. Transfer to the cooker. Add the onions and mushrooms.

Let the skillet cool, coat it with nonstick spray, and add the turkey. Brown it on both sides over medium-high heat, about 5 minutes. Transfer the turkey to the cooker.

Cover the cooker, lock lid into position, and place the pressure regulator on the vent pipe if you're using a first-generation cooker. Over medium-high or high heat, bring the cooker up to pressure. Reduce heat just enough to maintain pressure (regulator should rock gently), and cook the mixture for 10 minutes.

Let the pressure drop naturally for 5 minutes; then quick-release any remaining pressure (under cold running water if you're using a first-generation cooker). Carefully remove lid. Transfer the turkey and bacon to a platter, leaving the vegetables and broth in the cooker; keep the turkey warm.

Whisk together the cornstarch, pepper, thyme, celery seed and the remaining broth. Stir the cornstarch mixture into the vegetable–broth gravy. Cook, uncovered, until the gravy is thickened and hot, about 2 minutes.

Meanwhile, cook the noodles according to the package directions. Serve the turkey, bacon, and gravy over the noodles.

**Per serving:** 447 calories, 2.5 g fat (5% of calories), 0.7 g saturated fat, 102 mg cholesterol, 291 mg sodium, 3.1 g dietary fiber.

**Quick tip:** To wash mushrooms, wipe them with a damp cloth or quickly rinse them under cool running water. Never soak them; they become waterlogged easily.

# Turkey Vegetable Soup with Ditalini

*A frozen Italian-style vegetable mix cuts chopping time to practically nothing in this flavorful one-pot soup.*

## Makes: 4 servings

- 2 cans (14 ounces each) fat-free chicken broth or 3½ cups home-made stock
- ½ cup water
- 6 ounces boneless, skinless turkey breast, cut into ½-inch cubes
- 1 medium potato, cut into ½-inch cubes
- 2 cups frozen mixed Italian-style vegetables (a combination of broccoli, flat green beans, and zucchini)
- ½ teaspoon dried sage
- ¼ teaspoon freshly ground black pepper
- 1 cup ditalini

Combine the broth, water, turkey, and potato in a pressure cooker.

Place the lid on the cooker, lock it into position, and place the pressure regulator on the vent pipe if you're using a first-generation cooker. Over medium-high or high heat, bring the cooker up to pressure. Reduce heat just enough to maintain pressure (regulator should rock gently), and cook the mixture for 8 minutes.

Let the pressure drop naturally for 5 minutes; then quick-release any remaining pressure (under cold running water if you're using a first-generation cooker). Carefully remove the pressure regulator and lid. Stir in the mixed vegetables, sage, pepper, and ditalini. Place the lid loosely on the cooker (do not lock) and cook the soup over medium heat until the vegetables are tender and the ditalini are al dente, about 10 minutes.

**Per serving:** 233 calories, 0.8 g fat (3% of calories), 0.2 g saturated fat, 35 mg cholesterol, 190 mg sodium, 2.6 g dietary fiber.

**Quick tip:** In this recipe, you can peel the potatoes or simply give them a good scrubbing. The choice is yours to make.

# Vegetables Galore

## Black Bean and Corn Chili with Cheese Cornmeal Dumplings

*Create a stir with knockout chili that's full of beans and other healthful vegetables. Top with the best-ever one-step cornmeal dumplings.*

**Makes: 4 servings**

½ cup dried small red chili beans, soaked at least 1 hour in hot water

½ cup dried black beans, soaked at least 1 hour in hot water

1 can (28 ounces) tomatoes, cut up

1 large sweet green pepper, chopped

2 large onions, chopped

1½ cups corn

1 chili pepper, seeded and chopped

4 cloves garlic, minced

2 tablespoons chili powder

2 teaspoons ground cumin

1 teaspoon oregano

Cheese Cornmeal Dumplings (page 83)

Drain the chili beans and black beans and combine them in a pressure cooker; cover them with an inch of water.

Cover the cooker, lock the lid into position, and place the pressure regulator on the vent pipe if you're using a first-generation cooker. Over medium-high or high heat, bring the cooker up to pressure. Reduce heat just enough to maintain pressure (the regulator should rock gently), and cook for 4 minutes.

Quick-release the pressure (under cold running water if you're using a first-generation cooker). Carefully remove lid. Pour off the liquid and stir in the tomatoes, sweet peppers, onions, corn, chili pepper, garlic, chili powder, cumin and oregano.

Cover the cooker, lock the lid into position, and place the pressure regulator on the vent pipe if you're using a first-generation cooker. Over medium-high or high heat, bring cooker up to pressure. Reduce heat just enough to maintain pressure (regulator should rock gently), and cook for 2 minutes.

Meanwhile, prepare dumpling batter (see below).

Quick-release the pressure (under cold running water if you're using a first-generation cooker). Carefully remove the lid. Drop dumplings by the tablespoonfuls onto the hot chili. Loosely cover the cooker (do not lock the lid) and cook until the dumplings are done (a toothpick inserted in a dumpling should come out clean), 8 to 10 minutes.

**Per serving:** 491 calories, 8.2 g fat (14% of calories), 1.5 g saturated fat, 0.6 mg cholesterol, 179 mg sodium, 14.8 g dietary fiber.

**Quick tip:** Prefer not to spend time cooking beans? You can use canned instead, but be aware that the canned varieties will have more sodium. For this recipe, use one 15-ounce can each of red kidney and black beans. Be sure to rinse the beans thoroughly to remove as much surface sodium as possible. And skip the step for cooking the beans.

# Cheese–Cornmeal Dumplings

**Makes: 8 dumplings (4 servings)**

½ cup unbleached flour

½ cup cornmeal

1 teaspoon baking powder

2 tablespoons margarine

4 tablespoons shredded cheddar cheese

½ cup skim milk

Whisk together the flour, cornmeal, and baking powder. Using a pastry blender or two knives, cut in the margarine until the mixture resembles coarse crumbs. Stir in the cheese. Pour in the milk and mix, using a fork, until the ingredients are just combined. Drop onto the chili (see above).

**Per serving:** 187 calories, 6.2 g fat, 1.2 g saturated fat, 0.6 mg cholesterol, 145 mg sodium, 1.1 g dietary fiber.

# Border-Style Tortilla Soup

*I first sampled tortilla soup in Mexico City, and it was love at first spoonful. Since then, I've enjoyed it in several U.S. border cities. This version is topped with shredded Monterey Jack cheese, snipped parsley and crispy corn tortilla strips.*

### Makes: 6 servings

1 can (28 ounces) crushed tomatoes

1¼ cups reduced-sodium vegetable broth or homemade broth

2 onions, chopped

4 cloves garlic, chopped

1 chili pepper, minced

1 teaspoon ground cumin

2 tablespoons snipped fresh parsley

6 corn tortillas, cut into ¾-inch strips

nonstick olive-oil spray

1 cup shredded Monterey Jack cheese

Combine tomatoes, broth, onions, garlic, and pepper in a pressure cooker.

Place the lid on the cooker, lock it into position, and place the pressure regulator on the vent pipe if you're using a first-generation cooker. Over medium-high or high heat, bring the cooker up to pressure. Then lower the heat, adjusting it as necessary to maintain pressure (regulator should rock gently), and cook the soup for 4 minutes.

While the soup is cooking, place the tortillas on a baking sheet, and mist them with the olive-oil spray. Broil them until they're crisp and golden, 3 to 6 minutes.

Quick-release the pressure (under cold running water if you're using a first-generation cooker). Carefully remove the pressure regulator and lid. Stir in the cumin and parsley. Cook for 1 minute.

Divide the soup among 6 bowls, and top each serving with the tortilla strips and Jack cheese.

**Per serving:** 187 calories, 2.8 g fat (13% of calories), 0.9 g saturated fat, 7 mg cholesterol, 132 mg sodium, 4.3 g dietary fiber.

**Quick tip:** Have some baked tortilla chips in the pantry, but no corn tortillas? Coarsely break up the chips and top the soup with them instead of the tortilla strips.

# Butternut Squash and Apple Soup

*Here's a light soup with intriguing flavor contrasts—onion, apple, winter squash, and pumpkin pie spice—that's perfect for a spur-of-the-moment dinner. Serve it often in autumn when apples and squash are tiptop and plentiful.*

**Makes: 4 servings**

  4 potatoes (about 1½ pounds), peeled and cut into ¾-inch cubes

  1 butternut squash (about 1½ pounds), peeled and cut into ¾-inch pieces

  1 cup (1 large) McIntosh apple, peeled and coarsely chopped

  1 medium onion, chopped

  1 can (14 ounces) or 1¾ cup homemade reduced-sodium vegetable broth

  1 cup water

  1 teaspoon pumpkin pie spice

  ⅛ teaspoon white pepper

Combine the potatoes, squash, apples, onions, broth, and water in a pressure cooker.

Place the lid on the cooker, lock it into position, and place the pressure regulator on the vent pipe if you're using a first-generation cooker. Over medium-high or high heat, bring the cooker up to pressure. Reduce heat just enough to maintain pressure (regulator should rock gently), and cook the mixture for 5 minutes.

Quick-release the pressure (under cold running water if you're using a first-generation cooker). Carefully remove the pressure regulator and lid. Stir in the pumpkin pie spice and pepper; heat for 3 minutes to blend the flavors.

**Per serving:** 251 calories, 0.6 g fat (2% of calories), 0.1 g saturated fat, 0 mg cholesterol, 56 g sodium, 3.9 g dietary fiber.

**Quick tip:** Plumb out of pumpkin pie spice? No matter. In this recipe, you can substitute ½ teaspoon ground ginger and ¼ teaspoon ground nutmeg for the spice combo.

# French Onion and Mushroom Soup

*Many onion soup recipes require 45 minutes of simmering, too much time for my hectic schedule. This well-seasoned version takes just 5 minutes after your cooker pressures up.*

**Makes: 4 servings**

   1 teaspoon olive oil

   6 medium onions, quartered and sliced

   ¼ pound mushrooms, quartered

   2 cans (14 ounces each) fat-free beef broth or
      4 cups homemade stock

   2 cloves garlic, crushed

   ¼ cup dry red wine

   1 teaspoon dry mustard

   ⅛ teaspoon white pepper

   1 ounce Swiss cheese, shredded

   2 cups plain croutons

Pour the oil into a nonstick skillet, and warm it over medium-high heat. Working in batches, add the onions and mushrooms, and sauté them until golden, adding a teaspoon or so of broth at a time as necessary to encourage browning, about 15 minutes. Transfer the mixture to a pressure cooker. Add the broth, garlic, and wine to the cooker.

Place the lid on the cooker, lock it into position, and place the pressure regulator on the vent pipe if you're using a first-generation cooker. Over medium-high or high heat, bring the cooker up to pressure. Then lower the heat, adjusting it as necessary to maintain pressure (regulator should rock gently), and cook the mixture for 5 minutes.

Quick-release the pressure (under cold running water if you're using a first-generation cooker). Carefully remove the pressure regulator and lid. Stir in the mustard and pepper. Divide the soup among 4 soup bowls; top each serving with the shredded Swiss cheese and croutons.

**Per serving:** 197 calories, 4 g fat (18% of calories), 1.2 g saturated fat, 4 mg cholesterol, 259 mg sodium, 4.2 g dietary fiber.

**Quick tip:** You can make your own croutons if you have some dry Italian or French bread on hand. Simply cut the bread into ¾-inch cubes, mist them with olive-oil spray, and toast them under the broiler until golden, stirring occasionally to expose all sides.

# Italian-Style Vegetable–Pasta Stew

*This casual vegetarian dish is supercharged with flavor—thanks to rosemary and nutmeg.*

**Makes: 4 servings**

   olive-oil nonstick spray
   1½ cups quartered mushrooms
   3 cups reduced-sodium vegetable broth
   ½ cup dried black-eyed peas, soaked at least 1 hour in hot water
   3 carrots, sliced into ¾-inch pieces
   2 medium potatoes, cut into ¾-inch pieces
   1½ cups (2 ounces) rigatoni
   1 can (14 ounces) stewed tomatoes
   1½ teaspoons rosemary
   ⅛ teaspoon ground nutmeg
   2 cups torn spinach
   ¼ cup shredded Parmesan cheese

Coat a nonstick skillet with the spray and warm it over medium-high heat for 1 minute. Add the mushrooms, and sauté them until they're lightly browned. Transfer them to a pressure cooker. Add the broth, peas, carrots, and potatoes.

Place the lid on the cooker, lock it into position, and place the pressure regulator on the vent pipe if you're using a first-generation cooker. Over medium-high or high heat, bring the cooker up to pressure. Then lower the heat, adjusting it as necessary to maintain pressure (regulator should rock gently), and cook the mixture for 3 minutes.

Quick-release the pressure (under cold running water if you're using a first-generation cooker). Carefully remove the pressure regulator and lid. Stir in the rigatoni, tomatoes, rosemary, and nutmeg. Heat, uncovered, until flavors have blended and rigatoni are al dente, 16 to 20 minutes, stirring occasionally. Stir in the spinach, and cook the stew for 3 minutes. Ladle the stew into individual bowls. Top each serving with the Parmesan cheese.

**Per serving:** 267 calories, 2.3 g fat (8% of calories), 1.1 g saturated fat, 3.9 mg cholesterol, 413 mg sodium, 6.5 g dietary fiber.

**Quick tip:** For tasty beans with smooth skins, rinse and soak the beans in cold water for 8 to 20 hours before cooking them.

# Lombardy Minestrone

*Can a soup be hearty and have a delicate flavor at the same time? I think so. To be sure, why not stir up a potful of this Northern Italian minestrone with fresh vegetables and beans, and conduct your own taste test?*

**Makes: 4 servings**

1 medium potato, cut into ½-inch pieces

1½ cups green cabbage, coarsely chopped

1 stalk celery, chopped

1 carrot, sliced

4 plum tomatoes, chopped

2 cans (14 ounces each) fat-free chicken broth or 3½ cups home-made stock

1 small zucchini, quartered lengthwise and sliced

2 slices bacon, cooked and crumbled

1 medium red onion, chopped

½ cup snipped fresh basil leaves

1 can (16 ounces) cannellini beans, drained and rinsed

¼ teaspoon white pepper

Combine the potatoes, cabbage, celery, carrots, tomatoes, broth, zucchini, bacon, onion, basil, beans and pepper in a pressure cooker.

Cover the cooker, lock lid into position, and place the pressure regulator on the vent pipe if you're using a first-generation cooker. Over medium-high or high heat, bring the cooker up to pressure. Reduce heat just enough to maintain pressure (regulator should rock gently), and cook for 5 minutes.

Let pressure drop naturally for 10 minutes. Quick-release the remaining pressure (under cold running water if you're using a first-generation cooker). Carefully remove the pressure regulator and lid.

**Per serving:** 276 calories, 1.9 g fat (6% of calories), 0.6 g saturated fat, 3 mg cholesterol, 224 mg sodium, 11.2 g dietary fiber.

**Quick tip:** Fresh basil will stay perky for up to four days if you store it this way: Place the leaves, stems down, in a glass of water. Cover the leaves and glass with a plastic bag and refrigerate the whole thing.

# Potato Soup Monterey with Roasted Peppers

*This is one of my favorite quick and creamy soups. It's loaded with rich flavor and color, courtesy of Monterey Jack cheese and a smidgen of pureed carrot.*

**Makes: 6 servings**

6 large potatoes (about 2 pounds), peeled and cut into 1-inch pieces

1½ cups reduced-sodium vegetable broth or homemade stock

½ cup water

3 large scallions, white part, finely chopped

1 carrot, chopped

1 celery stalk, sliced

2 cloves garlic, pressed

⅛ teaspoon freshly ground black pepper

1 cup skim milk

1 cup shredded Monterey Jack cheese

½ cup canned roasted red peppers, chopped

parsley, garnish

Combine potatoes, broth, water, scallions, carrots, celery, and garlic in a pressure cooker.

Cover the cooker, lock lid into position, and place the pressure regulator on the vent pipe if you're using a first-generation cooker. Over medium-high or high heat, bring cooker up to pressure. Reduce heat just enough to maintain pressure (regulator should rock gently), and cook for 6 minutes.

Quick-release the pressure (under cold running water if you're using a first-generation cooker). Carefully remove the pressure regulator and lid. Using a potato masher, mash the vegetables, then whip them with a hand-held mixer or blender, stirring in the black pepper and milk. Stir in the cheese and red pepper, and cook until the cheese has melted, about 5 minutes. Divide the soup among 6 bowls; garnish each serving with the parsley.

**Per serving:** 202 calories, 2.3 g fat (10% of calories), 1 g saturated fat, 7 mg cholesterol, 97 mg sodium, 3.2 g dietary fiber.

**Quick tip:** Are you set on eating a soup with only 1 or 2 fat grams? Then switch to a nonfat cheese in this recipe. But take it from me: Nonfat won't impart the flavor or the creamy texture of a full-fat version.

# Red Bean, Rice and Shrimp Soup

*Goodness gracious, great bowls of flavor! Here, garlic, onions, chili powder, cumin, and lime power up the taste of familiar rice and beans.*

**Makes: 4 servings**

1 cup water

1 can (14 ounces) low-sodium vegetable broth or
   2 cups homemade stock

½ cup dried small red chili beans, soaked at least an hour

1 teaspoon olive oil

1 medium onion, chopped

1 clove garlic, crushed

¾ pound peeled and deveined shrimp

1 cup cooked long-grain rice

1 teaspoon chili powder

¼ teaspoon cumin seeds

1 can (14 ounces) stewed tomatoes

juice of 1 lime

Combine water, broth, beans, oil, onions, and garlic in a pressure cooker.

Place the lid on the cooker, lock it into position, and place the pressure regulator on the vent pipe if you're using a first-generation cooker. Over medium-high or high heat, bring the cooker up to pressure. Reduce the heat to just enough to maintain pressure (regulator should rock gently), and cook the mixture for 15 minutes.

Quick-release the pressure (under cold running water if you're using a

first-generation cooker). Carefully remove the pressure regulator and lid. Stir in the shrimp, loosely cover, and cook until shrimp are done, 5 to 8 minutes. Stir in the rice, chili powder, cumin, tomatoes, and lime juice. Loosely cover (do not lock lid) and cook until the flavors have blended and the soup is hot throughout, about 10 minutes.

**Per serving:** 312 calories, 3.2 g fat (9% of calories), 0.5 g saturated fat, 129 mg cholesterol, 385 mg sodium, 5.3 g dietary fiber.

**Quick tip:** No cooked rice on hand? Cook up a batch in a separate pot while the beans are cooking in the pressure cooker.

# Red Bean and Macaroni Soup

*This home-style dish is a meal in itself. It's lean; it's fast; it's delicious.*

**Makes: 6 servings**

- ½ cup water
- 2 cans (14 ounces each) fat-free chicken broth or 4 cups homemade stock
- ½ cup dried red beans, soaked at least 1 hour in hot water
- ¼ pound lean ham, cut into ¼-inch cubes
- 2 onions, chopped
- 1 celery stalk, chopped
- 4 cloves garlic, chopped
- 4 plum tomatoes, chopped
- ½ cup macaroni
- 1 teaspoon marjoram
- ⅛ teaspoon freshly ground black pepper
- 1 cup torn fresh mustard greens

Combine the water, broth, beans, ham, onions, celery, and garlic in a pressure cooker.

Place the lid on the cooker, lock it into position, and place the pressure regulator on the vent pipe if you're using a first-generation cooker. Over medium-high or high heat, bring the cooker up to pressure. Then lower the heat, adjusting it as necessary to maintain pressure (regulator should rock gently), and cook the mixture for 12 minutes.

Quick-release the pressure (under cold running water if you're using a first-generation cooker). Carefully remove the pressure regulator and lid. Stir in the macaroni, tomatoes, marjoram, and pepper. Cook the mixture for 3 minutes. Stir in the greens, and cook the soup for 3 minutes.

**Per serving:** 152 calories, 1.1 g fat (6% of calories), 0.2 g saturated fat, 3.1 mg cholesterol, 182 mg sodium, 4.7 g dietary fiber.

**Quick tip:** Add marjoram, a mild herb with an oreganolike flavor, to foods near the end of cooking; otherwise, its delicate essence may dissipate.

# Summer Vegetable Soup with Basil and Navy Beans

*Does your garden run over with summer squash and sweet peppers? Here's a super way to savor the bounty. Fresh basil complements the soup's flavor.*

**Makes: 4 servings**

1 cup small navy beans, soaked in hot water at least 1 hour

2 teaspoons olive oil

2 onions, cut into thin wedges

2 small (about 4 ounces each) zucchini, halved lengthwise and sliced ½ inch thick

2 small (about 4 ounces each) yellow squash, halved lengthwise and sliced ½ inch thick

4 cloves garlic, chopped

1 can (14 ounces) stewed tomatoes

1½ cup reduced-sodium vegetable broth or homemade stock

½ sweet red pepper, chopped

¼ teaspoon freshly ground black pepper

½ cup snipped fresh basil

Drain the beans and place them in a pressure cooker. Cover them with an inch of water and add 1 teaspoon of the oil (to keep the beans from foaming).

Place the lid on the cooker, lock it into position, and place the pressure regulator on the vent pipe if you're using a first-generation cooker. Over medium-high or high heat, bring the cooker up to pressure. Then lower the heat, adjusting it as necessary to maintain pressure (regulator should rock gently), and cook the beans for 9 minutes.

Meanwhile, place the remaining oil in a nonstick skillet and warm it over medium-high heat for 1 minute. Add the onions, zucchini, squash, and garlic, and sauté the vegetables until they're translucent.

Quick-release the pressure (under cold running water if you're using a first-generation cooker). Carefully remove the pressure regulator and lid. Drain the beans and return them to the cooker. Transfer the vegetables to the cooker. Add the tomatoes, broth, and sweet peppers.

Place the lid on the cooker, lock it into position, and place the pressure regulator on the vent pipe if you're using a first-generation cooker. Over medium-high or high heat, bring the cooker up to pressure. Then lower the heat, adjusting it as necessary to maintain pressure (regulator should rock gently), and cook the soup for 1 minute.

Quick-release the pressure under cold running water. Carefully remove the pressure regulator and lid. Stir in the black pepper and basil.

**Per serving:** 284 calories, 3.2 g fat (10% of calories), 0.5 g saturated fat, 0 mg cholesterol, 253 mg sodium, 15 g dietary fiber.

**Quick tip:** Fresh leafy herbs like basil are easy to cut if you stack them one atop another, roll them up lengthwise, then cut across the roll.

# Sweet Potato–Kielbasa Stew

*For assertive color, use the orange variety of sweet potatoes, sometimes mislabeled as yams, in this uncommonly good stew.*

### Makes: 4 servings

¼ pound lean turkey kielbasa, halved lengthwise
    and thinly sliced

1 pound sweet potatoes, peeled and cut into ¾-inch pieces

1 celery stalk, sliced

1 medium onion, chopped

1 parsnip, sliced into ½-inch pieces

1 can (28 ounces) stewed tomatoes

1 can (14 ounces) fat-free beef broth, or 2 cups homemade stock

1 medium potato, cut into 3- to 4-inch pieces

¼ teaspoon freshly ground black pepper

⅛ teaspoon ground nutmeg

2 tablespoons instant flour

Sauté the kielbasa in a nonstick skillet until lightly browned. Transfer it to a pressure cooker. Add sweet potatoes, celery, onions, parsnips, tomatoes, broth, and potatoes.

Place the lid on the cooker, lock it into position, and place the pressure regulator on the vent pipe if you're using a first-generation cooker. Over medium-high or high heat, bring the cooker up to pressure. Then lower the heat, adjusting it as necessary to maintain pressure (regulator should rock gently), and cook the mixture for 5 minutes.

Quick-release the pressure (under cold running water if you're using a first-generation cooker). Carefully remove the pressure regulator and lid. Stir in the pepper and nutmeg. Sprinkle the flour over the stew, and stir it in. Cook the stew until the sauce thickens, 2 to 3 minutes.

**Per serving:** 271 calories, 5.1 g fat (16% of calories), 1.3 g saturated fat, 18 mg cholesterol, 618 mg sodium, 5.3 g dietary fiber.

**Quick tip:** Parsnips are sweetest tasting in the fall and winter after the first frost of the season converts their starch to sugar.

# Vegetarian Sausage and Corn Chowder

*No question about it: The kernel is the ranking vegetable here. Roasted red peppers, vegetable-protein sausage, and hot-pepper sauce add pizzazz.*

**Makes: 4 servings**

nonstick spray

8 vegetable and grain protein sausage links, thawed and sliced ½-inch thick

1 cup reduced-sodium vegetable broth

2 potatoes, peeled and cut into ½-inch cubes

2 cups frozen corn

1 can (15 ounces) cream-style corn

½ cup thinly sliced scallions

½ cup chopped roasted red peppers

1 cup skim milk

1–2 teaspoons Louisiana hot-pepper sauce

Coat a nonstick skillet with the spray and warm it over medium-high heat for 1 minute. Add the sausage and cook it until lightly browned. Set it aside. Combine the broth and potatoes in a pressure cooker.

Place the lid on the cooker, lock it into position, and place the pressure regulator on the vent pipe if you're using a first-generation cooker. Over medium-high or high heat, bring the cooker up to pressure. Then lower the heat, adjusting it to maintain pressure (regulator should rock gently), and cook the mixture for 5 minutes.

Quick-release the pressure (under cold running water if you're using a first-generation cooker). Stir in the corn, cream-style corn, scallions, red peppers, and sausage. Cook the mixture until it's hot throughout and the corn is tender, about 5 minutes.

Pour the milk and hot-pepper sauce into the corn mixture, and cook the soup until it's thickened and hot throughout.

**Per serving:** 286 calories, 5.5 g fat (15% of calories), 1.2 g saturated fat, 1 mg cholesterol, 415 mg sodium, 7.8 g dietary fiber.

**Quick tip:** See the cautionary "quick tip" with the Black Bean and Ham Soup about using hot-pepper sauce.

# Braised Carrots and Leeks

*Braising, a simple technique that combines sautéing and simmering, imparts a mellow, nutty sweetness to these earthy vegetables.*

**Makes: 4 servings**

3 leeks, white part only, cut into ½-inch pieces

4 carrots, cut into ½-inch pieces

1 celery stalk, sliced diagonally into ½-inch pieces

1 teaspoon olive oil

1 tablespoon snipped fresh lemon thyme or 1 teaspoon dried

¼ cup dry white wine

½ cup low-sodium vegetable broth or homemade stock

freshly ground black pepper

In a large skillet, sauté leeks, carrots, and celery in oil over medium-high heat, about 5 minutes. Spoon the vegetables into a pressure cooker; add the thyme, wine, and broth.

Place the lid on the cooker, lock it into position, and place the pressure regulator on the vent pipe if you're using a first-generation cooker. Over medium-high or high heat, bring the cooker up to pressure. Then lower the heat, adjusting it as necessary to maintain pressure (regulator should rock gently), and cook the mixture for 30 seconds.

Quick-release the pressure (under cold running water if you're using a first-generation cooker). Carefully remove the pressure regulator and lid. Transfer the vegetables to a serving bowl and sprinkle them with the black pepper.

**Per serving:** 115 calories, 1.6 g fat (12% of calories), 0.2 g saturated fat, 0 mg cholesterol, 64 mg sodium, 4.1 g dietary fiber.

**Quick tip:** Leeks can be a sandy lot. To remove dirt trapped between layers, slit leeks from top to bottom and swish in plenty of cold water.

# Broccoli with Sesame Seeds

*Trying to bone up on calcium? These jazzed up spears offer a goodly amount (up to 5% of your daily requirement) of this important mineral.*

**Makes: 4 servings**

- ¾ pound broccoli spears
- ⅛ teaspoon freshly ground black pepper
- ½ teaspoon sesame oil
- 1 teaspoon toasted sesame seeds
- 1 teaspoon oregano

Pour 1 cup water into a pressure cooker. Place a rack or trivet in the bottom of the cooker. Place the broccoli on the rack.

Place the lid on the cooker, lock it into position, and place the pressure regulator on the vent pipe if you're using a first-generation cooker. Over medium-high or high heat, bring the cooker up to pressure. Immediately remove the cooker from the heat.

Quick-release the pressure (under cold running water if you're using a first-generation cooker). Carefully remove the pressure regulator and lid. Using a slotted spoon, transfer the broccoli to a serving bowl. Sprinkle the oil, seeds and oregano over the broccoli.

**Per serving:** 35 calories, 1.1 g fat (24% of calories), 0.1 g saturated fat, 0 mg cholesterol, 22 mg sodium, 2.7 g dietary fiber.

**Quick tip:** To toast sesame seeds, place them in a small nonstick skillet over medium-low heat. Warm them until they're golden, about 5 minutes, shaking the pan occasionally to redistribute the seeds.

# Butternut Squash and Onion Puree

*This unique pairing is just what the veggie meister ordered: a golden, palate-friendly dish that's 1-2-3 fast and easy.*

**Makes: 4 servings**

- ¾ cup fat-free chicken broth or homemade broth
- 1 onion, chopped
- 1 butternut squash, peeled and cut into 1-inch cubes
- 2 medium potatoes, peeled and cut into 1-inch cubes
- freshly ground black pepper

Combine the broth, onions, butternut squash, and potatoes in a pressure cooker.

Place the lid on the cooker, lock it into position, and place the pressure regulator on the vent pipe if you're using a first-generation cooker. Over medium-high or high heat, bring the cooker up to pressure. Then lower the heat, adjusting it as necessary to maintain pressure (regulator should rock gently), and cook the mixture for 5 minutes.

Quick-release the pressure (under cold running water if you're using a first-generation cooker). Carefully remove the pressure regulator and lid. Using a hand-held immersion blender, puree the squash–onion mixture. Top each serving with the pepper.

**Per serving:** 155 calories, 1.3 g fat (7% of calories), 0.3 g saturated fat, 0 mg cholesterol, 39 mg sodium, 1.9 g dietary fiber.

**Quick tip:** You can make this recipe even if you don't have a hand-held immersion blender. Simply use a potato masher or a hand-held mixer instead.

# Cauliflower with Chives and Cheddar

*This three-ingredient side dish is never fussy and always tasty.*

**Makes: 4 servings**

 ¾ pound cauliflower, broken into medium-size florets

 2 tablespoons shredded extra sharp cheddar cheese

 2 tablespoons snipped fresh or frozen chives

Pour water into a pressure cooker until it's 1 inch deep. Add a rack or trivet. Place the cauliflower on the rack.

Place the lid on the cooker, lock it into position, and place the pressure regulator on the vent pipe if you're using a first-generation cooker. Over medium-high or high heat, bring the cooker up to pressure. Then lower the heat, adjusting it as necessary to maintain pressure (regulator should rock gently), and cook the cauliflower 1 minute.

Quick-release the pressure (under cold running water if you're using a first-generation cooker). Carefully remove the pressure regulator and lid. Transfer the cauliflower to a serving bowl, and top the cauliflower with the cheddar and chives.

**Per serving:** 29 calories, 0.8 g fat (20% of calories), 0.2 g saturated fat, 1.2 mg cholesterol, 19 mg sodium, 2.3 g dietary fiber.

**Quick tip:** For maximum flavor and good melting, use freshly shredded cheese.

# Creamy Turnips with Cheese

*Delight family, friends, and finicky eaters with this smooth dish of potatoes, turnips, and two cheeses.*

**Makes: 4 servings**

1¼ cups fat-free chicken broth or homemade stock

1 pound turnips, peeled and cut into ½-inch pieces

1 pound potatoes, peeled and cut into ½-inch pieces

½ cup nonfat ricotta cheese

¼ cup shredded sharp cheddar cheese

¼ teaspoon white pepper

paprika, garnish

Combine the broth, turnips, and potatoes in a pressure cooker.

Place the lid on the cooker, lock it into position, and place the pressure regulator on the vent pipe if you're using a first-generation cooker. Over medium-high or high heat, bring the cooker up to pressure. Then lower the heat, adjusting it as necessary to maintain pressure (regulator should rock gently), and cook the mixture for 5 minutes.

Quick-release the pressure (under cold running water if you're using a first-generation cooker). Carefully remove the pressure regulator and lid. Using a potato masher, a hand-held immersion blender, or a hand-held mixer, mash the turnip–potato mixture, blending in the ricotta cheese, cheddar, and white pepper. Return the turnip–potato mixture to the heat and warm it, uncovered. Garnish each serving with the paprika and serve.

**Per serving:** 169 calories, 1.2 g fat (6% of calories), 0.5 g saturated fat, 5.3 mg cholesterol, 189 mg sodium, 4.3 g dietary fiber.

**Quick tip:** The peak season for turnips is October through February. To get young, tender, sweet-tasting turnips, look for small ones that are heavy for their size; oldsters tend to be large and woody with a strong flavor.

# Easy Orange-Glazed Carrots

*Got a bit of a sweet tooth? Then these baby carrots coated with a sweet marmalade glaze could make your day. A pinch of nutmeg lends spicy warmth to the glaze.*

**Makes: 4 servings**

- 2 cups water
- 1 package (16 ounces) baby carrots
- 2 tablespoons orange juice
- ¼ cup orange marmalade
- ⅛ teaspoon ground nutmeg

Pour the water into a pressure cooker. Add a rack or trivet. Place the carrots on the rack.

Place the lid on the cooker, lock it into position, and place the pressure regulator on the vent pipe if you're using a first-generation cooker. Over medium-high or high heat, bring the cooker up to pressure. Then lower the heat, adjusting it as necessary to maintain pressure (regulator should rock gently), and cook the carrots for 2 minutes.

Quick-release the pressure (under cold running water if you're using a first-generation cooker). Carefully remove the pressure regulator and lid. In a small microwave-safe bowl, mix the orange juice with the marmalade. Stir in the nutmeg. Microwave on medium until hot, 1 to 3 minutes.

Using a slotted spoon, transfer the carrots to a serving bowl. Pour on the marmalade mixture, and toss to coat the carrots.

**Per serving:** 108 calories, 0.3 g fat (2% of calories), 0.1 g saturated fat, 0 mg cholesterol, 46 mg sodium, 4.4 g dietary fiber.

**Quick tips:** For a sweeter glaze, add 1 teaspoon brown sugar to the marmalade mixture. Warming the orange juice and marmalade in a microwave makes it easy to blend the two ingredients. If you don't have a microwave, simply stir together the orange juice, marmalade, and nutmeg.

# Fast Parsley Potatoes

*Always popular and never a hassle, these potatoes will complement most meat, fish, or poultry main dishes.*

**Makes: 4 servings**

   1 cup fat-free chicken broth or homemade stock

   4 medium-large potatoes, cut into ¾-inch cubes

   1 teaspoon olive oil

   ¼ cup finely snipped fresh parsley

   ¼ teaspoon freshly ground black pepper

Combine the broth and potatoes in a pressure cooker.

Place the lid on the cooker, lock it into position, and place the pressure regulator on the vent pipe if you're using a first-generation cooker. Over medium-high or high heat, bring the cooker up to pressure. Then lower the heat, adjusting it as necessary to maintain pressure (regulator should rock gently), and cook the mixture for 6 minutes.

Quick-release the pressure (under cold running water if you're using a first-generation cooker). Carefully remove the pressure regulator and lid. Drizzle the oil over the potatoes. Top them with the parsley and pepper.

**Per serving:** 141 calories, 1.3 g fat (8% of calories), 0.2 g saturated fat, 0 mg cholesterol, 52 mg sodium, 2.7 g dietary fiber.

**Quick tip:** To snip parsley quickly, place it in a small cup. Then holding scissors with the blades pointed into the cup, snip, snip until the parsley is cut to the desired degree of fineness.

# Festive Braised Vegetables

*Here, six fresh vegetables—scallions, baby carrots, beets, turnips, green beans, and yellow squash—come together for a fast gourmet experience.*

**Makes: 4 servings**

- 2 teaspoons olive oil
- 8 scallions, cut into 3-inch lengths
- 16 baby carrots
- 4 beets, quartered
- 4 turnips, quartered
- 16 green beans, ends trimmed
- 1 small yellow squash, quartered lengthwise and crosswise
- 1 cup reduced-sodium vegetable broth, or homemade stock
- juice of 1 lemon
- ½ teaspoon freshly ground black pepper
- 1 tablespoon snipped fresh parsley

Place 1 teaspoon of the olive oil in a nonstick skillet and warm it over medium-high heat for 1 minute. Add half the scallions, carrots, beets, turnips, beans, and squash, and sauté for 3 minutes. Transfer vegetables to a pressure cooker. Place the remaining olive oil in the skillet, and sauté the remaining vegetables. Transfer to the cooker. Add the broth.

Place the lid on the cooker, lock it into position, and place the pressure regulator on the vent pipe if you're using a first-generation cooker. Over medium-high or high heat, bring the cooker up to pressure. Then lower the heat, adjusting it as necessary to maintain pressure (regulator should rock gently), and cook the mixture for 1 minute.

Quick-release the pressure (under cold running water if you're using a first-generation cooker). Carefully remove the pressure regulator and lid. Using a slotted spoon, transfer the vegetables to a serving bowl and sprinkle them with the lemon juice, pepper, and parsley.

**Per serving:** 98 calories, 2.6 g fat (21% of calories), 0.4 g saturated fat, 0 mg cholesterol, 103 mg sodium, 4.3 g dietary fiber.

**Quick tip:** Beet juice will initially give these vegetables a splash of red color. But don't worry. At the end of cooking, each vegetable will have retained its own identity and flavor.

# Garlic Mashed Potatoes

*Garlicky spuds like these are a hot item in trendy restaurants. But whipping them up is no big deal—when you use your pressure cooker.*

**Makes: 4 servings**

6 medium potatoes, peeled and quartered

8 cloves garlic, chopped

1 tablespoon minced dried onions

2 cups water

⅛ teaspoon white pepper

¾ cup milk

Combine potatoes, garlic, onions, and water in a pressure cooker.

Cover the cooker, lock lid into position, and place the pressure regulator on the vent pipe if you're using a first-generation cooker. Over medium-high or high heat, bring the cooker up to pressure. Reduce heat just enough to maintain pressure (regulator should rock gently), and cook for 6 minutes.

Quick-release the pressure (under cold running water if you're using a first-generation cooker). Carefully remove the pressure regulator and lid. Drain potatoes and transfer them to a bowl. Using a potato masher, mash potatoes with pepper and milk; finish by whipping them with an electric mixer, if desired.

**Per serving:** 203 calories, 0.3 g fat (1% of calories), 0.1 g saturated fat, 1 mg cholesterol, 39 mg sodium, 3.9 g dietary fiber.

**Quick tip:** Too rushed to peel and chop eight cloves of garlic? Use 4 teaspoons minced garlic from a jar instead.

# Pureed Sweet Potatoes

*This orange and sweet potato dish is simple, speedy and superb tasting–everything it should be. Try it tonight.*

**Makes: 4 servings**

4 sweet potatoes, peeled and cut into ¾-inch pieces

¾ cup orange juice

1 teaspoon grated orange peel

⅛ teaspoon white pepper

Combine potatoes and orange juice in a pressure cooker.

Place the lid on the cooker, lock it into position, and place the pressure regulator on the vent pipe if you're using a first-generation cooker. Over medium-high or high heat, bring the cooker up to pressure. Reduce heat just enough to maintain pressure (regulator should rock gently), and cook the potatoes for 7 minutes.

Quick-release the pressure (under cold running water if you're using a first-generation cooker). Carefully remove the pressure regulator and lid. Using a potato masher, mash the potatoes, or using a hand-held immersion blender, puree them. Stir in the orange peel and pepper.

**Per serving:** 231 calories, 4.7 g fat (17% of calories), 0.8 g saturated fat, 0 mg cholesterol, 106 mg sodium, 3.9 g dietary fiber.

**Quick tip:** When grating orange peel, use the colored part only. The white pith underneath is bitter.

# Quick Summer Squash Gratin

*Here, gratin, a toasted topping of crumbs and grated cheese turns garden-fresh squash into a proven-to-please side dish.*

**Makes: 4 servings**

- 1 pound small zucchini, sliced ¼ inch thick
- 1 pound yellow summer squash, sliced ¼ inch thick
- 1 cup vegetable broth
- ½ teaspoon olive oil
- ¼ cup seasoned bread crumbs, toasted
- 2 teaspoons Parmesan cheese
- ⅛ teaspoon freshly ground black pepper

Combine the zucchini, yellow squash, and broth in a pressure cooker. Place the lid on the cooker, lock it into position, and place the pressure regulator on the vent pipe if you're using a first-generation cooker. Over medium-high or high heat, bring the cooker up to pressure. Then lower the heat, adjusting it as necessary to maintain pressure (regulator should rock gently), and cook the mixture for 20 seconds.

Quick-release the pressure (under cold running water if you're using a first-generation cooker). Carefully remove the pressure regulator and lid. Using a slotted spoon, transfer the vegetables to a serving dish. Drizzle them with the oil, and top them with the bread crumbs, Parmesan, and pepper.

**Per serving:** 81 calories, 1.5 g fat (15% of calories), 0.4 g saturated fat, 0.8 cholesterol, 240 mg sodium, 1.4 g dietary fiber.

**Quick tip:** To toast the bread crumbs, place them in a small nonstick skillet. Warm them over medium heat, until they're golden brown, shaking the pan occasionally.

# Twice-Cooked Almond Potatoes

*Twice-baked potatoes, aka stuffed potatoes, was the inspiration for this smooth and rich side dish.*

**Makes: 4 servings**

1½ cup reduced-sodium vegetable broth or homemade stock

6 potatoes, peeled and cut into 1-inch pieces

⅔ cup shredded extra-sharp cheddar cheese

⅛ teaspoon white pepper

½ cup skim milk

nonstick spray

1 tablespoon sliced almonds

Combine the broth and potatoes in a pressure cooker.

Place the lid on the cooker, lock it into position, and place the pressure regulator on the vent pipe if you're using a first-generation cooker. Over medium-high or high heat, bring the cooker up to pressure. Then lower the heat, adjusting it as necessary to maintain pressure (regulator should rock gently), and cook the mixture for 8 minutes.

Quick-release the pressure (under cold running water if you're using a first-generation cooker). Carefully remove the pressure regulator and lid. Add the cheddar, pepper, and milk to the potatoes and, using a potato masher, mash the potatoes until they're smooth and fluffy.

Coat a 2-quart casserole with the nonstick spray. Spoon in the potato mixture, spreading it evenly. Top the potatoes with the almonds. Bake uncovered in a 350°F (177°C) oven until the potatoes are hot and the top of the casserole is lightly browned, 20 to 25 minutes.

**Per serving:** 419 calories, 4.8 g fat (10% of calories), 2.2 g saturated fat, 14 mg cholesterol, 163 mg sodium, 7.5 g dietary fiber.

**Quick tip:** Buy sliced almonds in little half-cup packages and stash what's left in the freezer, where they'll stay fresh for up to a year.

# Just Desserts

## Almond–Currant Applesauce

*As a self-professed fruit fanatic, I can't resist anything laden with apples, peaches, pears, or plums. This sweet treat is one of my favorite desserts. I think you'll find it very agreeable, too.*

**Makes: 4 servings**

4 McIntosh apples, quartered, cored and peeled

1 tablespoon lemon juice

1 tablespoon currants

1 tablespoon dark brown sugar

1 teaspoon ground cinnamon

1 tablespoon slivered almonds

1 cup apple juice

2 tablespoons maple syrup

Brush the apples with the lemon juice. Combine the apples, currants, sugar, cinnamon, and almonds in a pressure cooker.

Place the lid on the cooker, lock it into position, and place the pressure regulator on the vent pipe if you're using a first-generation cooker. Over medium-high or high heat, bring the cooker up to pressure. Reduce heat just enough to maintain pressure (regulator should rock gently), and cook the fruit for 3 minutes.

Let the pressure drop naturally. Carefully remove the pressure regulator and lid. Stir in the syrup.

**Per serving:** 158 calories, 1.6 g fat (8% of calories), 0.2 g saturated fat, 0 mg cholesterol, 5 mg sodium, 3.2 g dietary fiber.

**Quick tip:** Prefer a chunky sauce? Use Golden Delicious apples instead of the McIntosh, and cook them for just 2 minutes.

# Banana–Almond–Maple Custard

*It's a common dilemma: What to do with those overripe, brown-skinned bananas? Whisk up this sure-to-please custard with its own maple syrup sauce. For special occasions, dress it up even more with a garnish of fat-free whipped topping and freshly sliced bananas.*

**Makes: 4 servings**

butter-flavored nonstick spray

½ cup maple syrup

1 tablespoon sliced almonds

1 cup skim milk

⅓ cup sugar

1 cup mashed ripe banana (about 2 bananas)

1 egg

2 egg whites

1 teaspoon vanilla

Coat a heat-proof 1-quart dish with the spray. (The dish should fit inside your pressure cooker.) Tear off a 14 × 30 inch piece of heavy foil. Fold it in half lengthwise to make a 7 × 30 inch strip. Place the dish in the center of the strip. Pour the syrup into the dish. Sprinkle the almonds evenly over the syrup.

Blend the milk, sugar, banana, egg, egg whites and vanilla in a blender. Pour the custard mixture into the dish and cover the dish with a second piece of heavy foil.

Place a rack or trivet in the bottom of the pressure cooker. Pour in 2 cups of water. Bring the foil strip up, and fold it over the top of the dish. Using the strip to lower it, transfer the dish to the cooker. Leave the strip in place for cooking.

Place the lid on the cooker, lock it into position, and place the pressure regulator on the vent pipe if you're using a first-generation cooker. Over medium-high or high heat, bring the cooker up to pressure. Then lower the heat, adjusting it as necessary to maintain pressure (regulator should rock gently), and cook the custard for 15 minutes.

Let the pressure drop naturally. Carefully remove the pressure regulator and lid. Using the foil strip, carefully transfer the custard to a wire rack. Remove the foil covering and allow the custard to cool. Cover and refrigerate for at least 4 hours.

Using a knife or spatula, loosen the edges of the custard. Invert the custard onto a festive plate.

**Per serving:** 277 calories, 2.7 g fat (9% of calories), 0.7 g saturated fat, 54 mg cholesterol, 79 mg sodium, 1.6 g dietary fiber.

**Quick tip:** Ripe bananas, those with brown speckled skins, make the sweetest desserts. To mash them quickly, simply use the back of a fork.

# Butterscotch Pudding

*Sweet morsels aren't just for cookies: In this recipe, they form a melt-in-your-mouth base for a quick bread pudding.*

## Makes: 4 servings

butter-flavored nonstick spray

6 tablespoons butterscotch morsels

2 cups dry oat-bread cubes

1¼ cups skim milk

1 egg, slightly beaten

2 egg whites

¾ teaspoon vanilla extract

Coat a heat-proof 1-quart dish with the spray. (The dish should fit inside your pressure cooker.) Tear off a 14 × 30 inch piece of heavy foil. Fold it in half lengthwise to make a 7 × 30 inch strip. Place the dish in the center of the strip. Place the morsels and bread cubes in the dish.

In a bowl, whisk together the milk, egg, egg whites, and vanilla. Pour the mixture over the bread and morsels, and cover the dish with a seond piece of heavy foil.

Place a rack or trivet in the bottom of a pressure cooker. Pour in 2 cups of water. Bring the foil strip up and fold it over the top of the dish. Using the strip to lower it, transfer the dish to the cooker. Leave the strip in place for cooking.

Place the lid on the cooker, lock it into position, and place the pressure regulator on the vent pipe if you're using a first-generation cooker. Over medium-high or high heat, bring the cooker up to pressure. Then lower the heat, adjusting it as necessary to maintain pressure (regulator should rock gently), and cook the pudding for 15 minutes.

Let the pressure drop naturally. Carefully remove the pressure regulator and lid. Using the foil strip, carefully transfer the pudding to a wire rack. Remove the foil covering and allow the pudding to cool for 20 minutes. Serve warm.

**Per serving:** 174 calories, 6.5 g fat (34% of calories), 4.5 g saturated fat, 54 mg cholesterol, 167 mg sodium, 0.4 g dietary fiber.

**Quick tip:** Need some dry bread for this recipe? Simply pop 2 or 3 slices (that's all you'll need for 2 cups of bread cubes) into your toaster. Toast the bread until it's dry, but not brown, then cube the slices.


# Chocolate-Chip Cheesecake Dessert

*Chocoholics take note: This splendid dessert has a chocolate wafer crumb crust and tons of chocolaty chips in the rich-tasting creamy filling.*

**Makes: 4 servings**

   butter-flavored nonstick spray

   ½ cup reduced-fat chocolate wafer crumbs

   ¾ cup nonfat ricotta cheese

   ½ cup sugar

   6 tablespoons plain nonfat yogurt cheese

   2 tablespoons fat-free cream cheese

   1 egg

   1 tablespoon unbleached flour

   1 teaspoon vanilla

   ½ cup reduced-fat semisweet chocolate chips

Coat a heat-proof 1-quart dish with the spray. (The dish should fit inside your pressure cooker.) Tear off a 14 × 30 inch piece of heavy foil. Fold it in half lengthwise to make a 7 x 30 inch strip. Place the dish in the center of the strip. Press crumbs into the bottom of the dish.

Process the ricotta, sugar, yogurt cheese, cream cheese, egg, flour and vanilla in a food processor until just blended. With a rubber spatula, carefully fold in the chips. Pour the mixture into the dish and cover it with a scond piece of heavy foil.

Place a rack or trivet in the bottom of a pressure cooker. Pour in 2 cups of water. Bring the foil strip up and fold it over the top of the dish. Using the strip to lower it, transfer the dish to the cooker. Leave the strip in place for cooking.

Place the lid on the cooker, lock it into position, and place the pressure regulator on the vent pipe if you're using a first-generation cooker. Over medium-high or high heat, bring the cooker up to pressure. Then lower the heat, adjusting it as necessary to maintain pressure (regulator should rock gently), and cook the dessert for 12 minutes.

Let the pressure drop naturally for 5 minutes; then quick-release any remaining pressure (under cold running water if you're using a first-generation cooker). Carefully remove the pressure regulator and lid. Using the foil strip, carefully transfer the dessert to a wire rack. Remove the foil covering (set it aside) and allow the dessert to cool to room temperature. Cover and refrigerate at least 3 hours.

**Per serving:** 345 calories, 9.4 g fat (23% of calories), 7.6 g saturated fat, 58 mg cholesterol, 211 mg sodium, 0.9 g dietary fiber.

**Quick tip:** To make the yogurt cheese: Line a small colander or sieve with cheesecloth and set it over a deep bowl. Spoon ½ cup yogurt (it will reduce by approximately half) into the colander, cover the whole thing, and refrigerate it for 8 to 24 hours. When you're ready to use the cheese, discard the whey (the liquid in the bottom of the bowl) or save it to use in a soup or stew.

# Easy Gingered Pear Topping

*Here's a slightly spicy dried fruit sauce that's perfect atop nonfat vanilla frozen yogurt or angel food cake.*

**Makes: 6 servings**

  6 ounces dried pears, chopped

  3/4 cup currants

  1 cup apple juice

  1 tablespoon chopped crystallized ginger

Combine the pears, currants, juice, and ginger in a pressure cooker.

Place the lid on the cooker, lock it into position, and place the pressure regulator on the vent pipe if you're using a first-generation cooker. Over medium-high or high heat, bring the cooker up to pressure. Then lower the heat, adjusting it as necessary to maintain pressure (regulator should rock gently), and cook the fruit for 1 minute.

Let the pressure drop naturally. Carefully remove the pressure regulator and lid. Let mixture cool. Serve warm or chilled.

**Per serving:** 161 calories, 0.3 g fat (1% of calories), 0 g saturated fat, 0 mg cholesterol, 7.2 mg sodium, 3.4 g dietary fiber.

**Quick tip:** Use a sharp, heavy knife and a cutting board for chopping crystallized ginger.

# Maple–Pumpkin Custard

*Got a yen for pumpkin pie, but find that you have little time for preparing a crust? Satisfy that pumpkin craving with this snazzy custard. You'll never miss the crust. And here's a quick serving suggestion: Top the custard with lemon or vanilla low-fat yogurt or nonfat whipped topping.*

**Makes: 4 servings**

   butter-flavored nonstick spray

   1 cup canned pureed pumpkin

   ½ cup skim milk

   ⅓ cup dry milk powder

   1 egg

   1 egg white

   1 tablespoon unbleached flour

   2 tablespoons sugar

   2 tablespoons maple syrup

   1 teaspoon pumpkin pie spice

Coat a heat-proof, 1-quart dish with the spray. (The dish should fit inside your pressure cooker.) Tear off a 14 × 30 inch piece of heavy foil. Fold it in half lengthwise to make a 7 × 30 inch strip. Place the dish in the center of the foil strip.

Whisk together the pumpkin, milk, dry milk powder, egg, egg white, flour, sugar, maple syrup, and pumpkin pie spice. Pour the pumpkin mixture into the dish and cover it with a seond piece of heavy foil.

Place a rack or trivet in the bottom of a pressure cooker. Pour in 2 cups of water. Bring the foil strip up and fold it over the top of the dish. Using the strip to lower it, transfer the dish to the cooker. Leave the strip in place for cooking.

Place the lid on the cooker, lock it into position, and place the pressure regulator on the vent pipe if you're using a first-generation cooker. Over medium-high or high heat, bring the cooker up to pressure. Then lower the heat, adjusting it as necessary to maintain pressure (regulator should rock gently), and cook the custard for 15 minutes.

Let the pressure drop naturally for 5 minutes; then quick-release any

remaining pressure (under cold running water if you're using a first-generation cooker). Carefully remove lid. Using the foil strip, carefully transfer custard to a wire rack. Remove the foil covering and allow the custard to cool to room temperature.

**Per serving:** 132 calories, 1.6 g fat (10% of calories), 0.5 g saturated fat, 55 mg cholesterol, 80 mg sodium, 1.8 g dietary fiber.

**Quick tip:** If you have leftover canned pumpkin, freeze it in a tightly covered container. It'll keep for 3 to 4 months.

# Mandarin Orange Cheesecake Dessert

*Believe it. This wickedly delicious dessert, which features a gingersnap crust and refreshing mandarin orange topping, is really low fat and guilt free.*

**Makes: 4 servings**

butter-flavored nonstick spray

¼ cup gingersnap crumbs

¾ cup nonfat ricotta cheese

⅓ cup sugar

3 tablespoons plain nonfat yogurt cheese

2 tablespoons fat-free cream cheese

1 egg

1 tablespoon unbleached flour

½ teaspoon orange peel

Mandarin orange sections, drained, for garnish

Coat a heat-proof, 1-quart dish with the spray. (The dish should fit inside your pressure cooker.) Tear off a 14 × 30 inch piece of heavy foil. Fold it in half lengthwise into a 7 × 30 inch strip. Place the dish in the center of the strip. Press the crumbs into the bottom of the dish.

Process the ricotta, sugar, yogurt cheese, cream cheese, egg, flour and peel in a food processor until just blended. Pour the mixture into the dish and cover it with a second piece of heavy foil.

Place a rack or trivet in the bottom of a pressure cooker. Pour in 2 cups of water. Bring the foil strip up and fold it over the top of the dish. Using the strip to lower it, transfer the dish to the cooker. Leave the strip in place for cooking.

Place the lid on the cooker, lock it into position, and place the pressure regulator on the vent pipe if you're using a first-generation cooker. Over medium-high or high heat, bring the cooker up to pressure. Then lower the heat, adjusting it as necessary to maintain pressure (regulator should rock gently), and cook the dessert for 10 minutes.

Let the pressure drop naturally for 5 minutes; then quick-release any remaining pressure (under cold running water if you're using a first-generation cooker). Carefully remove the pressure regulator and lid. Using the foil strip, carefully transfer dessert to a wire rack. Remove the foil covering and allow the dessert to cool to room temperature. Cover and refrigerate at least 3 hours. Serve it garnished with the orange sections.

**Per serving:** 166 calories, 2.6 g fat (14% of calories), 0.8 g saturated fat, 57 mg cholesterol, 190 mg sodium, 0.1 g dietary fiber.

**Quick tips:** To make the yogurt cheese, see page 114. For a special occasion dessert try this: Prepare the dessert as in the recipe, but cook it in 4 six-ounce custard cups. Simply divide the mixture among the cups, stack them pyramid-style in the pressure cooker, and cook them for just 7 minutes. Cool as directed in the recipe. Right before serving, run a knife around the edge of each cup and unmold onto dessert plates.

# Poached Pears with Raspberry Glaze

*Here, I offer a 3-D dessert: delightfully easy, delightfully attractive, delightfully delicious. Serving suggestion: Top the pears with a dollop of vanilla low-fat yogurt.*

**Makes: 4 servings**

   6 cups cran-raspberry juice cocktail

   2 cups apple juice

   1 cinnamon stick

   2 lemon or orange tea bags

   4 firm Bosc or Anjou pears, peeled

   ¼ cup raspberry preserves, melted

Combine the juices, cinnamon, and tea bags in a pressure cooker. Submerge the pears in the juice mixture.

Place the lid on the cooker, lock it into position, and place the pressure regulator on the vent pipe if you're using a first-generation cooker. Over medium-high or high heat, bring the cooker up to pressure. Then lower the heat, adjusting it as necessary to maintain pressure (regulator should rock gently), and cook the fruit for 4 minutes.

Quick-release the pressure (under cold running water if you're using a first-generation cooker). Carefully remove the pressure regulator and lid. Discard the cinnamon stick and tea bags. Let the pears cool in the mulled juice. Using a slotted spoon, transfer the pears to dessert plates, reserving the mulled juice for another time, and drizzle the pears with preserves. Serve immediately.

**Per serving:** 146 calories, 0.7 g fat (4% of calories), 0 g saturated fat, 0 mg cholesterol, 8 mg sodium, 4.2 g dietary fiber.

**Quick tip:** The reserved cinnamon-raspberry poaching juice from this recipe makes for a singular sweet-tart mulled beverage. To serve it as a mid-afternoon pick-me-up, simply warm the juice on the stove top or in a slow cooker. Serve it in mugs, and use additional cinnamon sticks as stirrers.

# Quick Compote of Pears,
# Apricots and Cherries

*Somewhat tart and very satisfying, this dried fruit compote marries well with fruit sherbet and frozen yogurt.*

**Makes: 6 servings**

6 ounces dried pears

6 ounces dried apricots

½ cup dried cherries

½ cup dried cranberries

2½ cups cranberry juice

1 lime, sliced

1 cinnamon stick

⅛-inch-thick slice of gingerroot

Combine pears, apricots, cherries, cranberries and cranberry juice, lime slices, cinnamon stick and gingerroot in a pressure cooker.

Place the lid on the cooker, lock it into position, and place the pressure regulator on the vent pipe if you're using a first-generation cooker. Over medium-high or high heat, bring the cooker up to pressure. Then lower the heat, adjusting it as necessary to maintain pressure (regulator should rock gently), and cook the fruit for 4 minutes.

Quick-release the pressure (under cold running water if you're using a first-generation cooker). Carefully remove the pressure regulator and lid. Discard the cinnamon stick, lime slices, and gingerroot. Let cool. Serve the fruit warm or chilled.

**Per serving:** 237 calories, 0.7 g fat (3% of calories), 0 g saturated fat, 0 mg cholesterol, 9.3 mg sodium, 5.3 g dietary fiber.

**Quick tip:** Be sure to peel the gingerroot before adding it to the fruit mixture.

# Raisin Bread Pudding

*For a new take on bread pudding, try this one, which sports raisin bread, cinnamon and cardamom.*

**Makes: 4 servings**

butter-flavored nonstick spray

2 cups (about 4 slices) raisin bread cubes

¼ cup raisins

1 egg, slightly beaten

1 egg white

1¼ cups skim milk

¼ cup light brown sugar

¾ teaspoon vanilla extract

½ teaspoon cinnamon

⅛ teaspoon cardamom

Coat a heat-proof, 1-quart dish with the spray. (The dish should fit inside your pressure cooker.) Tear off a 14 × 30 inch piece of heavy foil. Fold it in half lengthwise into a 7 × 30 inch strip. Place the dish in the center of the strip. Place the bread and raisins in the dish.

In a bowl, whisk together the egg and egg white, milk, sugar, vanilla, cinnamon, and cardamom. Pour the milk mixture over the bread and raisins. Cover the dish with a second piece of heavy foil.

Place a rack or trivet in the bottom of the pressure cooker. Pour in 2 cups of water. Bring the foil strip up and fold it over the top of the dish. Using the strip to lower it, transfer the dish to the cooker. Leave the strip in place for cooking.

Place the lid on the cooker, lock it into position, and place the pressure regulator on the vent pipe if you're using a first-generation cooker. Over medium-high or high heat, bring the cooker up to pressure. Then lower the heat, adjusting it as necessary to maintain pressure (regulator should rock gently), and cook the pudding for 15 minutes.

Let the pressure drop naturally. Carefully remove the pressure regulator and lid. Using the foil strip, carefully transfer pudding to a wire rack. Remove the covering foil and allow the pudding to cool for 20 minutes. Serve warm.

**Per serving:** 152 calories, 2.6 g fat (15% of calories), 0.8 g saturated fat, 54 mg cholesterol, 171 mg sodium, 1.6 g dietary fiber.

**Quick tip:** You can use either raisin or cinnamon raisin bread in this recipe. It isn't necessary to pack the sugar when measuring.

# Rum-Raisin Rice Pudding

*Have you ever visited a gourmet confection shop and sampled rum-raisin ice cream? Then you know just how scrumptious the flavor can be. If you've never had it before, give it a try. You're sure to enjoy it.*

## Makes: 4 servings

butter-flavored nonstick spray

1½ cups cooked long-grain rice

½ cup golden raisins

1¼ cups skim milk

¼ cup light brown sugar

1 egg

2 tablespoons rum or 1 teaspoon rum extract

½ teaspoon vanilla extract

⅓ cup powdered skim milk

Coat a heat-proof, 1-quart dish with the spray. (The dish should fit inside your pressure cooker.) Tear off a 14 × 30 inch piece of heavy foil. Fold it in half lengthwise to make a 7 × 30 inch strip. Place the dish in the center of the strip.

Whisk together the rice, raisins, liquid skim milk, sugar, egg, rum, powdered skim milk and vanilla. Pour into the dish and cover it with a second piece of heavy foil.

Place a rack or trivet in the bottom of a pressure cooker. Pour in 2 cups of water. Bring the foil strip up and fold it over the top of the dish. Using the strip to lower it, transfer the dish to the cooker. Leave the strip in place for cooking.

Place the lid on the cooker, lock it into position, and place the pressure regulator on the vent pipe if you're using a first-generation

122

cooker. Over medium-high or high heat, bring the cooker up to pressure. Then lower the heat, adjusting it as necessary to maintain pressure (regulator should rock gently), and cook for 7 minutes.

Quick-release the pressure (under cold running water if you're using a first-generation cooker). Carefully remove the lid. Using the foil strip, carefully transfer the pudding to a wire rack. Remove the foil covering and stir the pudding. Allow the pudding to cool for 5 minutes. Stir in the powdered milk. Allow the pudding to cool to room temperature, stirring occasionally. Serve immediately or refrigerate.

**Per serving:** 265 calories, 1.7 g fat (6% of calories), 0.6 g saturated fat, 55 mg cholesterol, 93 mg sodium, 1 g dietary fiber.

**Quick tips:** If you prefer a thinner pudding, especially after it has been chilled, stir in additional skim milk, a little at a time.

# Spicy Pumpkin Cheesecake Dessert

*Smooth move. That's what tasters said about this delicious pairing of pumpkin and creamy cheese. I'm certain you'll happily agree.*

**Makes: 4 servings**

butter-flavored nonstick spray

½ cup gingersnap crumbs

¾ cup pureed cooked pumpkin

¾ cup nonfat ricotta cheese

½ cup light brown sugar

3 tablespoons plain nonfat yogurt cheese

2 tablespoons fat-free cream cheese

1 egg

1 tablespoon unbleached flour

1 teaspoon pumpkin pie spice

Coat a heat-proof, 1-quart dish with the spray. (The dish should fit inside your pressure cooker.) Tear off a 14 × 30 inch piece of heavy foil. Fold it in half lengthwise to make a 7 × 30 inch strip. Place the dish in the center of the strip. Press the crumbs into the bottom of the dish.

Process the pumpkin, ricotta, sugar, yogurt cheese, cream cheese, egg, flour and pumpkin pie spice in a food processor until just blended. Pour the mixture into the dish and cover it with a second piece of heavy foil.

Place a rack or trivet in the bottom of a pressure cooker. Pour in 2 cups of water. Bring the foil strip up and fold it over the top of the dish. Using the strip to lower it, transfer the dish to the cooker. Leave the strip in place for cooking.

Place the lid on the cooker, lock it into position, and place the pressure regulator on the vent pipe if you're using a first-generation cooker. Over medium-high or high heat, bring the cooker up to pressure. Then lower the heat, adjusting it as necessary to maintain pressure (regulator should rock gently), and cook the dessert for 15 minutes.

Let the pressure drop naturally. Carefully remove the pressure regulator and lid. Using the foil strip, carefully transfer dessert to a wire rack. Remove the foil covering (set it aside) and allow the dessert to cool to room temperature. Cover and refrigerate at least 3 hours.

**Per serving:** 215 calories, 3.7 g fat (15% of calories), 1.1 g saturated fat, 57 mg cholesterol, 232 mg sodium, 1.6 g dietary fiber.

**Quick tips:** To make the yogurt cheese, see page 114. Approximately 12 gingersnaps equal ½ cup crumbs.

# Easy Stocks

## Beef Stock

*A rich flavorful stock that's lean.*

**Yields: 9 cups**

2 ribs from roasted beef rib roast

2 celery stalks, leaves included, halved

4 large onions, with skins, quartered

4 medium carrots, halved

2 small turnips, quartered

2 bay leaves

8 whole black peppercorns

1 sprig parsley

1 sprig rosemary

10 cups water

Combine the beef and the celery, onions, carrots, turnips, bay leaves, peppercorns, parsley, rosemary, and water in a 6-quart (or larger) pressure cooker.

Place the lid on the cooker, lock it into position, and place the pressure regulator on the vent pipe if you're using a first-generation cooker. Over medium-high or high heat, bring the cooker up to pressure. Then lower the heat, adjusting it as necessary to maintain pressure (regulator should rock gently), and cook for 35 minutes.

Quick-release the pressure (under cold running water if you're using a first-generation cooker). Carefully remove the pressure regulator and lid. Pour the stock through a large strainer into a large bowl or pot. Discard the beef bones, vegetables and seasonings. Chill the stock, then skim off and discard the fat that's accumulated on the top of the liquid.

**Per cup:** 47 calories, 1 g fat (22% of calories), 0 g saturated fat, 0 mg cholesterol, 70 mg sodium, 0 g dietary fiber.

**Quick tip:** To store the stock, refrigerate it in covered containers for up to 3 days, or freeze it for up to 3 months.

# Chicken Stock

*A fast-to-make stock with only 1 gram of fat.*

**Yields: about 9 cups**

olive-oil nonstick spray

1 pound chicken breasts

2 celery stalks, leaves included, halved

4 large onions, with skins, quartered

4 medium carrots, halved

1 small turnip, quartered

2 bay leaves

8 whole black peppercorns

1 sprig parsley

1 sprig thyme

10 cups water

Coat a nonstick skillet with the spray and warm it over medium-high heat for 1 minute. Add the chicken and cook it until the pieces are browned on all sides. Transfer the chicken to a 6-quart (or larger) pressure cooker. Add the celery, onions, carrots, turnips, bay leaves, peppercorns, parsley, thyme, and water.

Place the lid on the cooker, lock it into position, and place the pressure regulator on the vent pipe if you're using a first-generation cooker. Over medium-high or high heat, bring the cooker up to pressure. Then lower the heat, adjusting it as necessary to maintain pressure (regulator should rock gently), and cook the mixture for 25 minutes.

Quick-release the pressure (under cold running water if you're using a first-generation cooker). Carefully remove the pressure regulator and lid. Pour the stock through a large strainer into a large bowl or pot. Discard the chicken bones, vegetables and seasonings; reserve the chicken breast meat for another use. Chill the stock; then skim off and discard the fat that's accumulated on the top of the liquid.

**Per cup:** 40 calories, 1 g fat (22% of calories), 0 g saturated fat, 0 mg cholesterol, 68 mg sodium, 0 g dietary fiber.

**Quick tip:** To store the stock, refrigerate it in covered containers for up to 3 days, or freeze it for up to 3 months.

# Turkey Stock

*A great way to use up leftover turkey wings.*

## Yields: about 9 cups

2 roasted turkey wings, skin included

2 celery stalks, leaves included, halved

3 large onions, with skins, quartered

2 medium carrots, halved

1 small turnip, quartered

1 parsnip

2 bay leaves

8 whole black peppercorns

1 sprig parsley

1 sprig sage

10 cups water

Combine the turkey, celery, onions, carrots, turnips, parsnip, bay leaves, peppercorns, parsley, sage, and water in a 6-quart (or larger) pressure cooker.

Place the lid on the cooker, lock it into position, and place the pressure regulator on the vent pipe if you're using a first-generation cooker. Over medium-high or high heat, bring the cooker up to pressure. Then lower the heat, adjusting it as necessary to maintain pressure (regulator should rock gently), and cook the mixture for 35 minutes.

Quick-release the pressure (under cold running water if you're using a first-generation cooker). Carefully remove the pressure regulator and lid. Pour the stock through a large strainer into a large bowl or pot. Discard the turkey, vegetables and seasonings. Chill the stock; then skim off and discard the fat that's accumulated on the top of the liquid.

**Per cup:** 45 calories, 1 g fat (22% of calories), 0 g saturated fat, 0 mg cholesterol, 55 mg sodium, 0 g dietary fiber.

**Quick tip:** To store the stock, refrigerate it in covered containers for up to 3 days, or freeze it for up to 3 months.

# Vegetable Stock

*The tastiest vegetable stock I've ever had, and it's exceptionally easy to make.*

### Yields: about 9 cups

4 large onions, quartered

4 medium carrots, halved

4 celery stalks, leaves included, halved

10 basil leaves

2 bay leaves

2 cloves garlic

8 whole black peppercorns

1 sprig parsley

10 cups water

Combine the onions, carrots, celery, basil leaves, bay leaves, garlic, peppercorns, parsley, and water in a pressure cooker.

Place the lid on the cooker, lock it into position, and place the pressure regulator on the vent pipe if you're using a first-generation cooker. Over medium-high or high heat, bring the cooker up to pressure. Then lower the heat, adjusting it as necessary to maintain pressure (regulator should rock gently), and cook the mixture for 12 minutes.

Quick-release the pressure (under cold running water if you're using a

first-generation cooker). Carefully remove the pressure regulator and lid. Pour the stock through a large strainer into a large bowl or pot. Discard the vegetables and seasonings.

**Per cup:** 43 calories, 0.2 g fat (4% of calories), 0 g saturated fat, 0 g cholesterol, 37 mg sodium, 0 g dietary fiber.

**Quick tip:** To store the stock, refrigerate it in covered containers for up to 3 days, or freeze it for up to 3 months.

# Glossary

**Allspice:** Though this spice tastes like a combination of cinnamon, nutmeg and cloves, it's really just one spice, a small, dark-brown berry. Allspice flavors both savory and sweet dishes, and you can buy it whole or ground.

**Balsamic vinegar:** Made from a very sweet grape and aged in wooden barrels for 10 years, balsamic vinegar tends to be sweeter and more expensive than most other vinegars. Dark brown in color with an exquisite mellow flavor, it complements delicate mixed greens salads.

**Black-eyed pea:** Also called a cowpea, this legume is small and beige with an oval black eye at the center of its curve. Its texture is mealy; its flavor, earthy. Look for black-eyed peas fresh, frozen, canned, or dried.

**Borscht:** a beet soup with origins in Russia and Poland, borscht usually contains meat and fresh vegetables and may be served either hot or cold with a dollop of sour cream.

**Butternut squash:** A variety of hard-shelled winter squash that has a beige exterior and a deep orange-colored flesh. Though generally available year round, butternut's peak season starts in early fall and ends in late winter. Purchase butternuts that are heavy for their size and blemish free. Since they don't need refrigeration, you can stash them in a cool, dry, dark spot for a month or more.

**Butterscotch:** This popular flavor comes from a blend of butter and brown sugar and is used to flavor confections and desserts as well as dessert sauces.

**Cacciatore:** An Italian-American dish that's prepared "hunter-style" with mushrooms, onions, tomatoes, herbs and chicken.

**Cannellini:** These are large white kidney beans popular in Italian soups and salads. They're available in dried and canned forms.

**Caper:** The flower bud of a Mediterranean shrub, the caper has a prized, sour and slightly bitter flavor. Its size ranges from tiny (a French nonpareil variety) to large (an Italian variety that's as big as the end of your little finger). Once picked, the bud is sun-dried, then packed in salt or a vinegar brine. To remove some of the saltiness, rinse in cold water before using them. The flower buds of nasturtium, buttercup, marigold and broom are sometimes used as inexpensive substitutes for capers.

**Caraway:** Small, crescent-shaped seeds with a delightful nutty, aniselike aroma and flavor. Used extensively in German and Austrian cooking. In the U.S., they're probably best known for flavoring rye bread.

**Chickpeas (garbanzo beans):** Round, tan legumes with a firm texture and mild, nutlike flavor. Used in Middle East dishes such as hummus (a garlic and lemon flavored dip). Available dried and canned.

**Chili powder:** A hot, spicy mixture of chili peppers, oregano, cumin, salt, garlic, coriander and cloves. For an intense blend, get one without salt. Chili powder is a mainstay in chilies and other Mexican and Tex-Mex-style dishes.

**Chinese wheat noodles:** Very thin noodles made from wheat, water, salt and, sometimes, eggs. The flavor is nutty and delicate. If you can't find them, substitute angel-hair pasta.

**Cider vinegar:** A mild, fruity vinegar made from fermented apple juice. Use it to add zing to slaws, vinaigrettes, vegetables, soups, stews and marinades.

**Celery seed:** Tiny pungent seeds of lovage, a cousin to celery. Its flavor is fairly intense, so use the spice, whole or ground, sparingly.

**Cilantro (Chinese parsley, fresh coriander):** Cilantro is an herb with small, fragile leaves and a lively, almost musty taste. It's a signature flavor for Caribbean, Latin American, and some Asian cuisines. Choose bunches of leaves with bright, lively color and no signs of wilting. Store cilantro, unwashed, in a plastic bag in the refrigerator for up to a week. Wash the leaves just before using them.

**Cloves:** The dried, unopened flower buds of a tropical evergreen tree, cloves are nail-shaped and have an intense, pungent flavor. Use cloves, which are available whole and ground, sparingly; their flavor can be overpowering. After cooking, discard whole cloves.

**Corned beef:** A cured beef product, either brisket or round, with a deep red color and a slightly salty taste. You can find ready-to-cook corned beef in your supermarket's meat section and cooked beef in the deli case.

**Cornmeal:** Resembling a coarse white- or yellow-colored flour, cornmeal is made from dried corn kernels. Used in corn bread, muffins, puddings, and polenta. If the package is labeled "stone-ground," expect a fairly coarse grind. You can store cornmeal in a tightly closed container in a cool dry place for up to 6 months, or in your refrigerator or freezer for up to a year.

**Cornstarch:** A white powdery thickener that leaves puddings, sauces, and gravies with a clear translucent appearance, making it a popular choice with many cooks. Cornstarch usually forms lumps when added to hot liquids. To prevent lumping, mix it with a little cold liquid before stirring it into the hot. To keep the sauce from thinning again, take care not to boil it or stir it too vigorously. Stored in a cool, dry place, cornstarch will keep for up to a year.

**Couscous:** A staple in several North African cuisines, couscous is a quick-cooking pasta made with semolina flour and water. To cook it, bring 2 cups of water or broth to a boil in a saucepan; stir in 1 cup of couscous; remove the pan from the heat. Allow the couscous to absorb the liquid for 5 minutes. Couscous is also the name of a dish in which cracked wheat is steamed over a simmering stew of chicken, raisins and chickpeas in a pot called a *couscoussière.*

**Cream-style corn:** When commercially prepared, this corn product contains corn, sugar and cornstarch. Homemade cream-style corn is the pulp and juice squeezed from corn kernels.

**Creole seasoning:** A zesty seasoning blend with three peppers—black, red and white—as well as several herbs and spices. Use it for the crusty, peppery seasoning on blackened catfish, as a spice rub for grilled meats or to perk up plain rice or pasta.

**Cumin:** A small, amber-colored seed resembling a miniature caraway seed, cumin has an aromatic, pungent—nutty flavor that dominates many Mexican and Indian dishes. You can find whole and ground cumin, a parsley relative, in most supermarkets. If you have access to an Asian market, check out the white and black cumin seeds. The white and amber varieties can be used interchangeably, but the black ones have a more complex, peppery flavor.

**Currants:** There are actually two fruits called currants: (1) a fresh, tiny berry in red, white, or black and (2) a tiny black seedless raisin. In this book, the currants used are the dried variety (raisins), which come from the Zante, or Corinth, grape. Use the dried variety as you would other raisins.

**Curry powder:** A blend of up to 20 spices and herbs including cumin, coriander, red pepper, fenugreek, cinnamon, allspice, fennel, ginger, black pepper, mace, nutmeg, cloves, poppy seeds, sesame seeds, and turmeric; the turmeric produces the yellow color. To eliminate any raw taste, toast curry powder in a small nonstick skillet before adding it to a recipe.

**Custard:** Made with sweetened milk and eggs, custards are silky, smooth puddinglike mixtures that take well be being dressed up with vanilla, chocolate, fruit purees and bits of nuts. But because milk and eggs dominate custards, the mixtures often curdle during cooking. To prevent curdling, always bake custards in a water bath (set the custard dish in a shallow pan of water) or steam them in a pressure cooker.

**Date:** A small golden brown to amber colored fruit that's extremely sweet. In the US, most dates are dried and are available whole (pitted or not) or chopped. Chopped dates are coated with sugar to keep them from sticking together. Store dried dates in an airtight container in a cool, dry place for up to 6 months or in the refrigerator for up to a year.

**Dill:** This name refers to both dillweed, the feathery leaves of the dill plant, and dillseed, the plant's tan, flat seeds. Both have a refreshing flavor, though dillseed is somewhat sharper. Whenever possible, use fresh dill for perking up salads, vegetables, sauces and viniagrettes; its flavor is superior to that of dried dillweed. Dillseed is best known for its use in pickling.

**Duck sauce:** A thick, sweet-sour condiment made with plums, apricots, sugar and seasonings. Often referred to as plum sauce and served with duck and pork.

**Ginger:** A seasoning with a somewhat sweet aroma, a pungent flavor, and a peppery after-kick, ginger comes in three forms: fresh (a gnarled root), dried and ground, and crystallized. Fresh ginger, often called gingerroot, makes a delicious contribution to curries, soups, and Asian-style stir-fries. Dried ginger, which should not be used as a substitute for the fresh version, adds indispensable flavor to gingerbread, gingersnaps, and ginger ale. Crystallized ginger, which has been cooked in a sugar syrup, jazzes up fruit compotes and the like. Fresh ginger can be stored, tightly wrapped in plastic wrap, in the refrigerator for up to 3 weeks or in the freezer for up to 6 months.

**Hoisin sauce:** This thick, sweet-spicy, reddish-brown condiment is widely used in Southern Chinese cooking. Its basic ingredients include soybeans, chili peppers, garlic, sugar, vinegar and spices. Hoisin sauce is available in Asian specialty groceries as well as many supermarkets. Once opened, it should be stored, tightly covered, in a glass jar in the refrigerator, where it'll keep for months.

**Hot pepper sauce:** Not a single sauce, but one of many Louisiana-style sauces made from hot chili peppers, vinegar and salt. The heat and flavor vary from brand to brand, some being relatively mild, others so scorching that just a drop or two fires up an entire dish. When using a hot sauce for the first time, cautiously add it to soups, stews, marinades and other dishes.

**Instant flour:** A specially formulated flour that dissolves quickly without lumping in hot and cold liquids. It's used mostly for thickening sauces and gravies.

**Italian herb seasoning:** A pleasant herb blend of oregano, basil and thyme, and sometimes red pepper, rosemary and garlic powder. Use the mix to achieve characteristic Italian flavor without measuring out the individual seasonings.

**Jambalaya:** One of Louisiana's most famous dishes, jambalaya is a variation of the Spanish paella. Though numerous versions exist (probably as many as there are cooks), most jambalayas contain rice, tomatoes, sweet peppers, chicken, sausage and/or ham as well as seafood.

**Kale:** A nonheading member of the cabbage family that grows best in cooler climates, kale has dark green frilly leaves and a mild cabbage flavor. You can serve it raw or cooked in any manner you might prepare spinach. Just be sure to remove and discard the tough center stems. To buy kale, look for crisp, deeply colored leaves. Store kale in the refrigerator for up to 3 days.

**Kielbasa:** This is a robust smoked Polish sausage that's usually sold pre-

132

cooked. Most kielbasa, also known as kielbasy, is made with pork, though beef is sometimes added. Nowadays, you can also get lower-fat turkey versions. For best flavor, always heat kielbasa before serving it.

**Lemon pepper:** A seasoning blend of black pepper and grated lemon zest. Check the label before buying this blend; it sometimes contains more salt than pepper or lemon.

**Lentils:** Meaty tasting and packed with protein, lentils are small disk-shaped legumes that come in three varieties: greyish-brown (European), reddish-orange (Egyptian) and yellow. The greyish-brown are commonly found in supermarkets; the others can be obtained in Middle Eastern and Indian groceries. Stored at room temperature in a dry place, lentils will keep for a year.

**Mandarin oranges:** These are a variety of oranges with thin, loose skins and easily separated segments. You can find fresh mandarin oranges under the names tangerines and tangelos. Canned mandarin oranges are usually a different variety: small Japanese satsuma oranges, which are seedless.

**Maple syrup:** The boiled and concentrated sap of the maple tree. In the U.S., the syrup is graded. Grade AA (Fancy) has a mild flavor and a light, delicate color; Grades A and B are a little less refined; and Grade C is the least refined, with a very dark color and a robust, almost molasseslike flavor. Maple-flavored and pancake syrups both contain lots of corn syrup and little or no real maple syrup, and cost far less than the real thing. After opening pure maple syrup, store it in the refrigerator.

**Marjoram:** Also called sweet marjoram. A member of the mint family, marjoram has long, oval leaves with a mild oreganolike flavor. To retain its delicate taste, add it to dishes toward the end of cooking.

**Marmalade:** A jamlike spread with a sweet–tart character, marmalade is made from a citrus fruit, usually oranges, bits of its peel and sugar. Marmalades make enticing glazes for roasted meats and poultry and cooked vegetables.

**Mustard greens:** These dark leafy greens, popular in Southern country cooking, have a pungent, almost peppery mustard flavor, and provide a tasty accent to green salads and cooked dishes. For top quality, buy them during their peak season: December through March. Look for small crisp leaves with a bright color. To store them, place them in a plastic bag in the refrigerator for up to a week. Rinse and pat them dry immediately before use.

**Mustard seeds:** Seeds of the mustard plant, a peppery green belonging to the same family as broccoli, Brussel sprouts, kale, collards, and kohlrabi. The seeds themselves come in three varieties: black, brown, and yellow. Yellow is the most common. Left whole or cracked, mustard seeds boost the flavor of potato salad, pickles, relishes, and boiled shrimp.

**Nutmeg:** A hard, brownish seed with a warm, spicy, sweet flavor. It's sold ground and whole; expect to get the best flavor from freshly ground whole nutmeg. Use nutmeg to perk up baked goods, quiches, custards, and vegetables, such as potatoes and winter squash.

**Paprika:** A special variety of red sweet pepper pods, ground for use as a seasoning and a garnish. Paprika comes from several parts of the world—Spain, California, South America and Hungary. The Hungarian variety is considered by many to be a standout. After opening paprika, store it in the refrigerator where it'll retain its bright color and flavor longest.

**Pasta:** A dough (or paste) made with flour and water and, sometimes, eggs. Generally speaking, pasta made with eggs is called noodles in the United States. You can make your own pasta or buy it fresh, frozen or dried, the latter being the most popular since it's inexpensive and keeps almost indefinitely. Dried pasta comes in at least 600 shapes.

**Pearl onions:** Small (less than an inch in diameter) onions with a mild flavor. Often creamed, and also favored in pickled condiments.

**Picadillo:** A Hispanic dish that includes ground meat, tomatoes, garlic, onions and other local ingredients. In Cuba, picadillo is often served with black beans and rice.

**Piccata:** A simple Italian dish that's made with sautéed veal or chicken, topped with a lemon-and-parsley sauce.

**Peppercorn:** The berries of the pepper plant *(Piper nigrum)*, which produces black and white pepper. Black pepper, the most popular, comes from the dried berry with its skin; white pepper, which is also dried, comes minus the skin. Of the two, white pepper is slightly milder and is a good choice in light-colored sauces where dark specks of black pepper would stand out.

**Peppers**: Crunchy, colorful, flavorful, sweet, hot, versatile, high in vitamin C—such attributes make peppers a favored vegetable in many cuisines: Mexican, Chinese, Thai, Hungarian, to name a few. Though there are scads of pepper varieties, all can be divided into two basic categories—sweet and hot. Here's a brief rundown of several popular and readily available peppers:

> **Anaheim:** A long, slender, moderately hot pepper that's also known as New Mexican, long green, long red or California. They're the pepper of choice in the classic Mexican dish, *chiles rellenos.*
>
> **Bell:** A sweet, bell-shaped pepper that comes in green, red, yellow, orange, brown or purple. Suitable for stuffing, slicing and dicing; use to punch up color, flavor and crunch in a soup, stew, casserole, stir-fry or sandwich.
>
> **Cayenne:** A long, thin, sharply pointed hot pepper, either straight or curled. Generally sold when fully ripe and red in color.
>
> **Cubanel (cubanelle):** A long (about 4 inches from tip to core), tapered pepper, also known as an Italian frying pepper. Light green or yellow, cubanels are mild but more flavorful than bells and are great for cutting into long thin strips for sautéing.
>
> **Jalapeño:** A tapered, 2-inch-long, very hot pepper, usually sold at the green, but mature, stage. Used to season sausages, cheeses, even jellies.

**Pimento (pimiento):** A large, heart-shaped, mild pepper, usually sold in jars. Thick and meaty, fresh pimentos are ideal for roasting.

**Poblano:** A very dark green, moderately hot pepper that resembles a small bell pepper with a tapered blossom end.

**Pollo:** This means chicken in Italian and Spanish.

**Pumpkin pie spice:** A blend of four spices: cinnamon, ginger, nutmeg, and allspice. Use it to pump up the flavor of baked goods and simple savory dishes.

**Ricotta cheese:** "Ricotta" means recooked in Italian. Made from a combination of cooked whey (a by-product of cheesemaking and, hence, the term recooked) and milk, ricotta is a white, moist fresh cheese. It often serves as the filling in savory dishes, such as lasagna and stuffed shells, and in desserts, such as cheesecake.

**Rosemary:** The green leaves of this aromatic herb resemble pine needles, and many cooks describe its taste as somewhat piny. Chop fresh leaves before using them and crush the dried form in a mortar and pestle. Rosemary is fairly assertive, especially when fresh, so apply it with restraint in vinaigrettes, sauces, lamb and chicken dishes.

**Sesame oil:** Pressed from sesame seeds, sesame oil comes in two types: light and dark. The light oil is lighter in flavor and color; use it to enhance salad dressings and for sautéing. Use the dark oil for accenting Asian dishes.

**Shallot:** Related to onions, shallots look more like giant brown garlic bulbs. A shallot bulb is composed of multiple cloves, each covered with a thin, dry, papery skin. Choose those that are plump and firm with no signs of wilting or sprouting. Keep in a cool, well-ventilated spot for up to a month. Mild in flavor, shallots can be used in the same manner as onions.

**Smoke flavoring:** Available in liquid form, smoke flavoring is nothing more than smoke concentrate in a water base.

**Soy vegetable crumbles:** Developed as meatless alternatives to ground beef, these tasty, low-fat (but not necessarily low-sodium) products are made with soy protein and seasonings.

**Tarragon:** An herb popular in French cooking, with a distinctive, almost licoricelike taste. Tarragon's slender, pointed and dark green leaves flavor such dishes as chicken, Béarnaise, and fines herbes. Use with a little caution; its assertiveness can easily overwhelm other flavors.

**Tortilla:** Made from corn (masa) or wheat flour, tortillas are thin, flat, round unleavened Mexican breads that resemble pancakes. Traditionally, they're fried on a griddle. Tortillas can be eaten plain or wrapped around a multitude of fillings to create tacos, burritos, enchiladas, tostadas and chimichangas. Store prepackaged tortillas according to package directions.

**Turmeric:** Probably best known for the bright yellow color it gives American-style prepared mustards, turmeric is a musty, bittersweet spice related to ginger. Use this dried powder sparingly; it's pretty intense stuff—so intense that it will stain plastic utensils. Turmeric is an inexpensive substitute for saffron.

**Water chestnut:** Crisp, white fleshed and very low in fat and calories, water chestnuts give stir-fries and other Asian dishes a welcome juicy crunch. These chestnut look-alikes are actually the edible tubers of a water plant from Southeast Asia. They're available fresh in Asian specialty groceries and canned in most supermarkets. Peel fresh water chestnuts before using them.

**Wild pecan rice:** This is a delightful aromatic rice, sometimes labeled simply pecan rice, that hails from Louisiana. It has a wonderful nutty flavor, and the grains remain fluffy and separate after cooking.

**Wine vinegars:** Mildly zesty vinegars made from red or white wines. Use to make simple vinaigrettes and other salad dressings as well as marinades.

**Worcestershire sauce:** A dark, pungent condiment made from soy sauce, vinegar, garlic, tamarind, onions, molasses, lime, anchovies, and other seasonings, Worcestershire sauce was first concocted in India and bottled in Worcestershire, England. Use it to flavor soups, meats, gravies, and vegetable juices.

# Emergency Substitutes

Uh-oh, you've checked the pantry and looked in the refrigerator, so there's no doubt about it: you're out of nonfat sour cream, Italian herb seasoning and chili powder. Three ingredients your favorite recipe calls for, and you planned to serve the recipe tonight. What now? Check this handy table; it'll help you find quick replacements for missing items. Just remember, the substitutes may give the recipe a somewhat different flavor or texture.

| Recipe Requires | Quick Substitute |
|---|---|
| Bacon (1 slice crumbled) | Bacon bits (1 T) |
| Allspice | Cinnamon; dash of nutmeg |
| Bread crumbs, dry (1 cup) | Cracker crumbs (¾ cup) |
| Broth, beef or chicken (1 cup) | Bouillon cube (1) plus boiling water (1 cup) |
| Chili powder (1 T) | Hot-pepper sauce (a drop or two) plus oregano (¼ tsp) and cumin (¼ tsp) |
| Cinnamon (1 tsp) | Allspice (¼ tsp) or nutmeg (¼ tsp) |
| Cornstarch (1 T) | All-purpose flour (2 T) |
| Cumin (1 tsp) | Chili powder (1 tsp) |
| Egg (1 whole) | Egg substitute (¼ cup) |
| Flour, as thickener (2 T) | Cornstarch (1 T) or quick-cooking tapioca (2 T) |
| Garlic (1 clove) | Garlic powder (⅛ tsp) |
| Ginger (1 tsp) | Allspice (½ tsp), cinnamon (1 tsp), or nutmeg (½ tsp) |
| Italian herb seasoning (1 tsp) | Basil, dried (1 tsp) plus thyme, dried leaves (1 tsp) |
| Lemon juice (1 tsp) | Cider vinegar (½ tsp) |
| Lemon peel (1 tsp grated) | Lemon extract (½ tsp) |
| Mustard, dry (1 tsp) | Mustard, prepared (1 T) |
| Nonfat sour cream (1 cup) | Plain nonfat yogurt (1 cup) |
| Onion (1 minced) | Onions, dried, minced (1 T) |
| Pumpkin pie spice | Cinnamon, ground (1 tsp) plus nutmeg, ground (½ tsp) and powdered ginger (½ tsp) |
| Seasoned bread crumbs, dry (1 cup) | Plain dry bread crumbs (⅞ cup) plus grated Parmesan cheese (1 T) and dried parsley (1 T) |
| Sherry (1 T) | Sherry extract (1 T) |
| Teriyaki sauce (1 T) | Soy sauce (1 T) plus powdered garlic (⅛ tsp) and minced fresh ginger (¼ tsp) |
| Tomato sauce (1 cup) | Tomato paste (½ cup) plus water (½ cup) |
| Vinegar (1 tsp) | Lemon juice (2 tsp) |

Key to abbreviations: T = tablespoon; tsp = teaspoon

# Culinary Math

Quick, quick! A creamy soup recipe calls for 1 cup of broccoli florets. How many pounds of fresh broccoli should you buy? A stew requires 2 cups of beef broth. How many cans should you open? Stumped? That's understandable. After all, who among us memorizes such nitty-gritty food facts? For an approximate answer (it's impossible to be exact), look to this concise table.

## A

**Almonds, shelled, blanched:** ½ pound = 1½ cups whole = 2 cups slivered

**Apples:** 1 pound = 3 medium = 2¾ to 3 cups chopped or sliced

**Apricots, dried:** 1 pound = 2¾ cups = 4½ to 5½ cups cooked

**Asparagus, fresh:** 1 pound = 16 to 20 spears

**Asparagus, frozen, cut:** 1 package (10 ounces) = 2 cups

## B

**Bananas:** 1 pound = 3 to 4 medium = 2 cups sliced = 1¾ cups mashed

**Beans, green, fresh:** 1 pound = 3½ cups whole

**Beans, green, frozen:** 1 package (9 ounces) = 1½ cups

**Beans, kidney, canned:** 16 to 17 ounces = 2 cups

**Beans, kidney, dried:** 1 pound = 2½ cups = 5½ cups cooked

**Beans, navy, dried:** 1 pound = 2⅓ cups = 5½ cups cooked

**Beef broth:** 1 can (14 ounces) = 1¾ cups

**Beef, cooked, cubed:** 1 cup = 6 ounces

**Beef, ground:** 1 pound = 2 cups uncooked

**Beets, fresh, without tops:** 1 pound = 2 cups chopped

**Bread:** 1 slice fresh = ½ cup soft crumbs = ¼ to ⅓ cup dry crumbs

**Broccoli, fresh:** 1 pound = 2 cups chopped

**Broccoli, frozen:** 1 package (10 ounces) = 1½ cups chopped

**Brussels sprouts, fresh:** 1 pound = 4 cups

## C

**Cabbage:** 1 pound = 3½ to 4½ cups shredded = 2 cups cooked

**Carrots, fresh:** 1 pound without tops = 3 cups chopped or sliced = 2½ to 3 cups shredded; 1 medium = ½ cup chopped or sliced

**Carrots, frozen:** 1 package (1 pound) = 2½ to 3 cups sliced

**Cauliflower:** 1 pound = 1½ cups small florets

**Celery:** 1 stalk = ½ cup chopped or sliced

**Cheese–blue, feta, gorgonzola:** 4 ounces = 1 cup crumbled

**Cheese–cheddar, Monterey Jack:** 1 pound = 4 cups shredded or grated

**Cheese–Parmesan, Romano:** 4 ounces = 1 cup shredded or grated

**Chicken, cooked, cubed:** 1 cup = 6 ounces

**Chicken broth:** 1 can (14 ounces) = 1¾ cups

**Corn, fresh:** 2 to 3 ears = 1 cup kernels

**Corn, frozen:** 1 package (10 ounces) = 1¾ cups kernels

**Cornmeal:** 1 pound dry = 3 cups uncooked = 12 cups cooked

## E

**Egg, large:** 1 yolk = 1 tablespoon; 1 white = 2 tablespoons

**Egg, large:** 7 to 8 = 1 cup

**Eggplant:** 1 pound = 3 to 4 cups diced

**Egg substitute:** ¼ cup = 1 whole egg; 1 package (8 ounces) = 1 cup = 4 whole eggs

## G

**Garlic:** 2 medium cloves = 1 teaspoon minced

## H

**Herbs–basil, cilantro, dill, parsley, thyme:** 1 tablespoon, fresh, chopped = 1 teaspoon dried

## L

**Lemon:** 1 medium = 2 to 3 teaspoons grated peel and 3 tablespoons juice; 1 pound = 4 to 6 medium lemons = 1 cup juice

**Lime:** 1 medium = 1 teaspoon grated peel and 2 tablespoons juice; 1 pound = 6 to 8 medium limes = ⅓ to ⅔ cup juice

## M

**Macaroni:** 1 pound = 4 cups dry = 8 cups cooked

**Mushrooms, fresh:** ½ pound = 2½ to 3 cups sliced = 1 cup sliced sautéed

## N

**Noodles:** 1 pound = 6 cups dry = 7 cups cooked

## O

**Okra, fresh:** 1 pound = 2 cups sliced

**Onion:** 1 medium = ½ cup minced = ¾ to 1 cup chopped

**Orange:** 1 medium = 2 tablespoons grated peel and ⅓ cup juice; 1 pound = 3 medium = 1 cup juice

**P**

**Parsnips:** 1 pound = 4 medium = 2 cups chopped
**Peas, frozen:** 1 package (10 ounces) = 2 cups
**Peas, in pod:** 1 pound = 1 to 1½ cups shelled
**Peppers:** 1 medium sweet = 1 cup chopped
**Potatoes, sweet:** 1 pound = 3 medium = 3½ to 4 cups cubed or sliced = 2 cups mashed
**Potatoes, white:** 1 pound = 3 medium= 3½ to 4 cups cubed or sliced = 2 cups mashed

**R**

**Rice, brown:** 1 cup uncooked = 4 cups cooked
**Rice, white:** 1 cup uncooked = 3 cups cooked

**S**

**Scallions:** 2 medium, white part only = 1 tablespoon
**Scallions:** 2 medium with green tops = ¼ cup
**Spinach, fresh:** 1 pound = 8 to 10 cups torn
**Squash, yellow or zucchini:** 1 pound = 3 medium = 2½ cups sliced
**Squash, winter:** 1 pound = 1 cup mashed

**T**

**Tomato, fresh:** 1 medium = ½ cup chopped; 1 pound = 3 large = 4 medium = 1½ cups chopped
**Tomatoes, canned:** 1 can (28 ounces) crushed = 3¾ cups

**Y**

**Yogurt:** ½ pint = 1 cup = 8 ounces

# Culinary Abbreviations

| | | |
|---|---|---|
| **t** = tsp = teaspoon | **lb** = pound | **mL** = milliliter |
| **T** = tbsp = tablespoon | **g** = gram | **F** = Fahrenheit |
| **c** = cup | **kg** = kilogram | **C** = Celsius |
| **oz** = ounce | **mg** = milligram | |
| **fl oz** = fluid ounce | **L** = liter | |

# Everyday Equivalents

Recalling most measures—for example, 8 ounces equal a cup and others we use everyday—is a snap. But those used once a decade (at least it seems that seldom) easily slip our minds. To jog your memory and help you measure up, refer to this table of U.S. to metric equivalents, rounded for easy use.

| U. S. UNITS | | | METRIC |
|---|---|---|---|
| **LIQUIDS** | | | |
| ¼ teaspoon | | | 1 milliliter |
| ½ teaspoon | | | 2 milliliters |
| 1 teaspoon | 60 drops | ⅙ fluid ounce | 5 milliliters |
| 1 tablespoon | 3 teaspoons | ½ fluid ounce | 15 milliliters |
| 2 tablespoons | ⅛ cup | 1 fluid ounce | 30 milliliters |
| 4 tablespoons | ¼ cup | 2 fluid ounces | 60 milliliters |
| 5⅓ tablespoons | ⅓ cup | 2⅔ fluid ounces | 80 milliliters |
| 8 tablespoons | ½ cup | 4 fluid ounces | 113 milliliters |
| 1 cup | 16 tablespoons | 8 fluid ounces | 236 milliliters |
| 2 cups | 1 pint | 16 fluid ounces | 500 milliliters |
| 4 cups | 1 quart | 32 fluid ounces | 1 liter |
| 4 quarts | 1 gallon | 128 fluid ounces | 3¾ liters |

| TEMPERATURE | | WEIGHT | |
|---|---|---|---|
| 32°F | 0°C | 1 ounce | 28.35 grams |
| 212°F | 100°C | 4 ounces | 115 grams |
| 350°F | 177°C | 8 ounces | 225 grams |
| 400°F | 205°C | 16 ounces (1 pound) | 454 grams |
| 450°F | 233°C | 32 ounces (2 pounds) | 907 grams |
| | | 36 ounces (2¼ pounds) | 1000 grams |

# Index